No-Sweat Desktop Publishing

No-Sweat Desktop Publishing

A Guide From Home Office Computing *Magazine*

Steve Morgenstern

AMERICAN MANAGEMENT ASSOCIATION

New York • Atlanta • Boston • Chicago • Kansas City • San Francisco • Washington, D.C.
Brussels • Toronto • Mexico City

This publication is designed to provide accurate and authoritative information in regard to the subject matter covered. It is sold with the understanding that the publisher is not engaged in rendering legal, accounting, or other professional service. If legal advice or other expert assistance is required, the services of a competent professional person should be sought.

Library of Congress Cataloging-in-Publication Data

Morgenstern, Steve.
    No-sweat desktop publishing / Steve Morgenstern.
        p. cm.
    Includes index.
    ISBN 0-8144-7729-1
    1. Desktop publishing.   I. Title.
    Z286.D47M67 1992   92-5247
    686.2'2544—dc20   CIP

Printing number

10 9 8 7 6 5 4 3 2 1

For my parents,
Lila and Sy Morgenstern,
who don't much care about computers,
but like to see their son's byline anyway.

CONTENTS

8. Newsletters   137

News Reporting • Browsable Material • Information
Worth Keeping • Encourage Action • Newsletter Design
Guidelines • A Step-by-Step Newsletter Project •
Newsletter Design Ideas

9. Flyers and Brochures   151

A Question of Attitude • Keep It Simple • Flyer and
Brochure Design Ideas

10. A Mixed Bag   159

Reports and Proposals • Report and Proposal Design
Ideas • Résumés • Résumé Design Ideas • Business Forms •
Business Form Design Ideas • Letterhead and Business
Cards • Letterhead and Business Card Design Ideas •
Overheads • Overhead Design Ideas • Space
Advertisements • Space Advertisement Design Ideas

11. Getting It Printed   169

The Tail That Wags the Dog • Explaining What You
Need • Creating Mechanicals • Looking Sharp With
Imagesetter Output • Choosing a Service Bureau •
Working With a Service Bureau • Preparing Your
Mechanicals • Communicating Through
Your Mechanical • Tints, Screens, and Spot Color

12. If I Knew Then...   193

Index   199

No Sweat? No Kidding!

Desktop publishing isn't about computers — it's about communicating your message more effectively.

This is a book about communication.

It deals with the computers and the technology and the terminology and the procedures you'll need to become a desktop publisher.

But first, last, and foremost, it is a book about communication. Because you're not interested in mastering desktop publishing for the sheer joy of learning to use a powerful technology. You want to acquire the means to communicate more effectively.

And part of what is intriguing about desktop publishing is the fact that the form of the communication you create with your computerized tools is entirely traditional. Desktop publishing has not changed the shape or feel or form of the final output in significant ways. The book you are holding was created using desktop publishing technology. Twenty years ago, when I took my first job in book publishing, the same book could have been created using non-computer means, and it would be pretty near impossible to tell the difference between the two.

The difference is not in the output created but in the process of creation. As a young editor working in a publishing house I handled one aspect of the book-creating process — whipping the words into shape. I then handed those words over to a designer, who worked with a typesetter and a pasteup artist to turn that raw material into a ready-for-the-printing-press book. Even today, designers, typesetters, and pasteup artists have their place in professional publishing. But if I want to, for reasons of control, or budget, or personal expression, I can use the power of desktop publishing to do a credible job on my own, without outside assistance, at lower cost and without sacrificing quality.

I've been doing this for years now, but the process never fails to amaze me.

An Enabling Technology

Computers are sometimes called "an enabling technology," a phrase I've always liked. The computer enables you to take the talents at your command and use them more productively, removing barriers and enhancing capabilities.

Cost is certainly a barrier to effective communication — if it's going to cost thousands of dollars to prepare a flyer to promote your business, you're not going to do it. By adopting desktop publishing, though, you may reduce those thousands to a few hundred and get the flyer out the door.

Desktop publishing saves money by eliminating several expensive and time-consuming steps from the traditional production process. For example, a friend of mine is a professional designer and a self-confessed computerphobe. When he wants to create a brochure, he sends the text to a typesetter who *retypes it all!* In addition to the time consumed and the errors introduced in the process, this is simply a waste of money when compared to a desktop publishing system that takes the original manuscript as saved in a word-processing file and uses it to generate typeset pages.

Similarly, when my friend gets his type back from the outside typesetting house, a professional mechanical artist must laboriously position it in camera-ready form for the print shop. Desktop publishers perform that task on the computer, once again saving time and money.

Of course, there are barriers to adopting desktop publishing in the first place. There is the initial financial investment in computer

The technology of midrange desktop publishing lets you send a powerful message to your audience, even if you aren't a publishing professional.

hardware and software. And there's the investment of time and effort in learning how to use the stuff.

Something wonderful has happened in the past year or so, though, that is really the inspiration for this book. The twin barriers of high initial investment and steep learning curve have both been lowered dramatically.

A New Generation of Software

We usually think of evolution as a process where simple organisms develop into more complex creatures, but desktop publishing has "evolved" from the complex to the simple. Thanks to software that streamlines the design process, the businessperson who can communicate verbally can now go on to the next step — producing publications that present information in a graphically exciting and impressive form.

For several years there were two tiers of desktop publishing software — the high-end, expensive, complex programs developed to serve the needs of publishing professionals, and the low-end, amateur tools that were supposed to be good enough for basic publishing tasks.

The problem was, the low-end tools were lousy. They were awkward to use, unable to handle basic publishing chores (such as hyphenating text), and produced low-quality printouts that looked shabby compared to materials produced using traditional publishing processes.

Recently, however, a tremendous resource became available with the release of a new generation of midrange desktop publishing programs. The designers of these new programs have combined ease of use with an impressive level of polish and precision to create a superb opportunity for desktop publishing "wannabes." What's more, even the best of the midrange programs sell for one-quarter to one-third the cost of high-end desktop publishing software.

While the software side of desktop publishing saw the introduction of low-cost, low-intimidation programs, prices for computer hardware with enough power to handle real-world desktop publishing projects have plummeted. Apple Computer adopted more aggressive pricing strategies, and the fiercely competitive world of IBM PC-compatibles now offers high-powered computers at prices that would have been literally unbelievable a few short years ago. And the same more-bang-for-the-buck pricing trend is also evident when shopping for the other key component of your desktop publishing system, a laser printer.

Defining "No-Sweat" Desktop Publishing

What do I mean by "no-sweat" desktop publishing? I mean an experience distinctly different from my own introduction to desktop publishing, which must honestly be described as high-sweat.

I was working as a freelance writer with a variety of corporate accounts.

A client hired me to write and edit a newsletter. I asked if he'd like me to carry the job a step further and produce final camera-ready pages for delivery to the print shop. I explained that, with this new desktop publishing stuff, I could do it all on my computer, cut down on the time it would take to produce the job, and give him a better price than someone using traditional production techniques. He bought it.

Of course, I knew desktop publishing could do all that because I had been eagerly following all the computer magazines and gazing longingly at the laser printers at my local computer dealer's show-room. But that didn't mean I had ever tackled a desktop publishing project myself. What had I gotten myself into?

As it turned out, I had gotten myself into a very lucrative extension of my writing business. But I had also gotten in way over my head.

I went out and bought a laser printer and an accelerator card for the PC I already owned, plus an expensive high-end desktop publishing program. Add the cost of the three together and I saw much of my fee for this project consumed in a flash. My forehead began to grow moist.

Then, with a deadline staring me in the face, I sat down to learn how to set up the hardware and use the software. The beads of sweat on my forehead developed into rivulets, leaving little puddles of panic on the pages of that software manual. And I was an experienced editor who knew something about how publications were produced!

I should have given myself more time to get up and running

before promising to deliver the goods to my client. But beyond that, I was sweating because of limitations in the desktop publishing process — limitations that have since been eliminated. The equipment and the software required were expensive. Today they aren't. The software was difficult to understand and to use. Now it isn't. And, in that early stage of desktop publishing, I didn't have anybody around to explain the ins and outs to me in a comprehensible, no-nonsense way.

Now you do.

Setting Achievable Goals

This book provides all the information you need to put together a simple, yet powerful, desktop publishing system and use it to produce professional-looking newsletters, brochures, catalogs, flyers, and other forms of business communication — and it does all that in about 200 pages.

The key to accomplishing so much so quickly is to narrowly focus our efforts on the goal at hand and to eliminate much that is historical, theoretical, "artistic," and/or overly advanced. Basic, straightforward publications can be powerful business tools, whether your audience is a group of customers, or prospective customers, or readers of the Loyal Order of Raccoons newsletter.

By "basic," I don't mean we're going to abandon the pursuit of quality. Far from it! In fact, I'll explain in some detail the procedures needed to go beyond laser printer output and achieve the same high-resolution standards produced by traditional typesetting using your desktop publishing system.

My goal is, quite simply, to help you reach your goal — to communicate effectively through desktop publishing technology. And we can do that "quite simply" without sacrificing that all-important professional polish.

I'm not saying this is a "no-brains" undertaking.

I'm not saying it's "no-talent."

But if you have the basic smarts, the ability to communicate your ideas in words, and enough design sense to distinguish the good from the bad and the ugly, you can become an effective desktop publisher.

No sweat.

You don't have to be artistically inclined to master desktop publishing.

ACKNOWLEDGMENTS

Since 1985, *Home Office Computing* magazine (née *Family Computing*) has played a significant role in both my professional life and my personal life.

As an author, it has given me the opportunity to explore technologies that intrigue me, and write about them not as a computer scientist but as an enthusiastic user.

And as a home-based worker, the magazine has provided the non-alcoholic equivalent of the bar in *Cheers* — a warm, friendly place where everybody knows your name. This book, which brings together much of my work on the subject of desktop publishing, seems an appropriate place to thank the entire staff, past and present, for making me feel that I truly have a home at *Home Office*.

Nick Sullivan, Senior Editor at the magazine, generously offered his valuable insight in shaping this book. Myles Thompson, Acquisitions Editor at AMACOM, made me an offer I couldn't refuse by suggesting the project. I thank them both.

My most profound gratitude as a writer trying to make a living in the computer field goes to David Hallerman, my long-suffering editor at *Home Office Computing*. A good editor is a rare and valuable commodity, combining a certain persnickety exactitude with the ability to offer constructive suggestions and an appreciation for what makes a given writer's prose distinctive. On that basis David is a very good editor indeed. I value him highly both as a professional colleague and as a friend.

Finally, thanks to my wife, Helen, and my kids, Jason and Jessica. Without their unflagging support, I would never be able to handle the intimidating task of facing a blank computer screen every morning and trying to make prose.

CHAPTER 1

The Business Side of Desktop Publishing

Not long ago I received a letter from a consultant in Buffalo who went shopping for easy-to-use desktop publishing software at her local computer store. "I have to say I was impressed with the copy on the box that says: 'You can be publishing in an hour!'" she wrote. "Well, if there were ever jail sentences that could be given out by consumers for false advertising…this one should land the whole bunch of them in the slammer for a long time."

I'm with you! So let me be frank right up front. Even if we stick to the basics, you'll need a few thousand dollars' worth of computer hardware and software (though you may already own all you need). You'll certainly have to invest some time mastering new software and new techniques and be willing to accept a challenge. I said desktop publishing can be a "no-sweat" proposition, and it can. I never said it could be grasped instantaneously.

In fact, it's a good thing desktop publishing isn't *too* easy. If it were, then anybody could do it. Think back to the first word-processed computer-printed letters you received. Pretty impressive, right? Today we take that level of communication for granted. In fact, you *have* to employ word-processing technology today just to be average.

There is still an opportunity to be distinctive by adopting desktop publishing technology, however. Today a reasonably intelligent person can master basic desktop publishing techniques in a reasonably brief period of time. And for your time and trouble, you gain a powerful communications capability that can set you apart from your competitors in dramatic ways.

HIGH QUALITY, LOW PRICE

What makes desktop publishing distinctive is the level of quality you can achieve with little or no outside assistance, at an economical price. Using my computer with a laser printer and a little ingenuity, I can produce an array of printed materials ranging from books and magazines to stuff-under-windshields-at-the-shopping-center flyers. Most man-on-the-street recipients find laser-printed output as impressive as publications created the old-fashioned way using professional typesetters. And for those with a more discerning eye, a desktop publisher can spend a few extra dollars to output pages on high-resolution typesetting equipment. At that point, even persnickety types like myself can't tell the difference between the results produced by desktop publishing and traditional techniques.

A David-and-Goliath Technology

Desktop publishing is a true David-and-Goliath technology. Those of us whose offices used to be spare bedrooms generally don't have the resources of "the big boys," yet often that's precisely whom we're competing against for customers and clients.

Bob Little of Blue Sky Design Corporation in Miami used desktop publishing to create a complete kit to support an insurance company client's Spanish-language marketing program. Shown here are the cover (above) and one inside page (right) from a 4-fold, 3-color brochure.

UniLife Two

REGLAS DEL ASEGURADOR

1. Cuando la cantidad excede los $500,000.00, el examen deberá ser hecho por un cardiologo o por un especialista en medicina interna.

2. Cuando existan problemas renales cardiovasculares o historia de diabetes en la familia se requerira un examen de orina.

Valor Nominal	Edades de Emisión						Requisitos Adicionales
	0-35	36-45	46-50	51-55	56-60	61-65	66+
50,000-75,000	A	A	B	B	B	B	C	
75,001-100,000	A	B	B	B	B	C	1a
100,001-150,000	B	B	B	C	D	E	1
150,001-200,000	B	B	C	D	D	D	E	1
200,001-250,000	C	C	C	E	E	E	E	1,4a
250,001-300,000	C	C	D	E	E	E	E	1,3,4
300,001-350,000	C	C	E	E	E	E	E	1,3,4
350,001-500,000	D	D	E	E	E	E	E	1,3,4,5a
500,001-999,999	E	E	E	E	E	E	E	1,3,4,5
1,000,000-mas	E	E	E	E	E	E	E	1,2,3,4,5

A = Sin Examen Médico
B = Examen Médico
C = Examen Médico y de Orina
D = Examen Médico, Orina y Electrocardiograma
E = Examen Médico, Orina, Electrocardiograma y Rayos X

1 = Reporte de Agente
1a = Reporte de Agente para $100,000.00
2 = Reporte de Inspección
3 = Examen de S.I.D.A.
4 = Informe Confidencial y Personal
4a = Informe Confidencial y Personal para $250,000.00
5 = Reporte Financiero
5a = Reporte Financiero para $500,000.00

La compañía se reserva el derecho de solicitar requisitos adicionales si así fuera necesario.

High-quality desktop publishing output helps close the gap by delivering your message with professional crispness and style.

You may be a one-person accounting firm preparing a proposal for a prospective client who is considering both large and small firms.

Or maybe you're building a lawn-care business and want a brochure that looks good when a homeowner weighs it against the slick promotional materials produced by your corporate franchised competition.

Or maybe you work at a major corporation and need to create an internal newsletter yourself, with no budget to tap outside resources. David-and-Goliath struggles are waged every day within corporations, as each departmental fiefdom attempts to reach its own goals and achieve recognition. And the ability to communicate more powerfully through desktop publishing is as valuable to the individual with entrepreneurial spirit competing within the corporate world as it is to the one-man-shop entrepreneur attempting to drum up business for a kitchen-table-based new venture.

BUSINESS APPLICATIONS

There are really three sides to small-business desktop publishing:

- Professional publishing of books, newsletters, and other materials to be sold commercially;
- Creating materials that attract and retain customers for your nonpublishing business;
- Selling your services as a desktop publisher who creates printed materials for others.

How do the advantages of desktop publishing create business opportunities in each of these areas?

PROFESSIONAL PUBLISHING

In professional publishing, the answer is too obvious to linger on. To a large extent, desktop publishing has been adopted as standard procedure throughout the publishing industry, including magazines, newspapers, book publishing, and advertising. Increasingly, publishing professionals are pushing the boundaries of desktop publishing to include reproducing four-color photographs (creating color separations) in-house.

The entrepreneur who dreams of creating a publication of his or her own will inevitably see desktop publishing as a godsend. Having run the figures for my own start-up publication ideas more than once, I'd advise caution. Desktop publishing drastically cuts the cost of preparing publication pages. It does nothing to cut paper, printing, and mailing costs, or the cost of acquiring subscribers.

Which is not to say out of hand that your idea for a great new newsletter won't make you rich. If you know a great deal about a specific area of interest (generally the more specialized, the better), have access to "inside information," or can otherwise make your publication stand out from the pack and have enough capital to bring your brainchild to the attention of prospective customers, work out a business plan incorporating desktop publishing technology. It will keep your initial production costs down and make it easy to produce a timely, up-to-the-minute publication.

As a sidelight, keep in mind the possibility of delivering your publication via fax. Fax publishing is becoming increasingly popular with audiences who demand the fastest possible receipt of vital information. It is also an attractive option for those who are geographically remote and receive mail slowly but have access to a phone line and a fax machine.

The mechanics of desktop-publishing the pages of your publication are essentially unchanged if it is going to be delivered via fax, though you will have to take the delivery method into account at the design stage to minimize small-size typefaces and illustrations that reproduce poorly when faxed.

When it comes to sending your faxed publication to subscribers, you may be able to improve reproduction quality by sending the actual publication file using a fax modem with your computer. In addition to eliminating the reproduction quality loss inherent in the process of scanning a page into a fax machine, a fax board can also be programmed to send identical pages to a number of different telephone numbers automatically, redialing if necessary until the connection is made.

PROMOTING YOUR BUSINESS

Most of the samples and advice in this book will focus on using desktop publishing to promote your nonpublishing business.

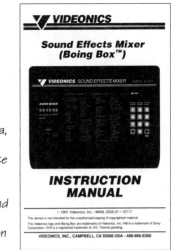

Videonics in Campbell, California, uses desktop publishing to create everything from promotional brochures (left) and magazine ads to product instruction manuals (right).

The low-cost aspect of desktop publishing allows you to increase the volume of communication with clients and potential clients. Basic advertising smarts tell you that the impression you make on an audience is governed in large measure by the *recency* and *frequency* of your contact with them. With desktop publishing, frequent contact becomes a more economically viable strategy.

Mail order marketing is a perfect example of a business where frequent contact often spells higher profits. You want to be there for the customer at the moment when he or she needs your goods or services. The mailing you sent a month ago is probably now cozily nestled in a landfill somewhere. What if that prospect now wants to respond to your offer? He or she is waiting to hear from you again (or from your competitor).

Frequent contact is one strategy made more attractive through desktop publishing; strategic contact is another. If you order anything from a smart mail order marketer, you'll find more than the goods you ordered in the box when it arrives. You'll find some form of communication — perhaps a thank-you note for your order, or an offer of additional products with a bounceback order form, or a discount coupon to be applied toward your next purchase. Each of these "supplemental" publications can lead to additional business either right away or at a later date. And because these additional solicitations tag along with the product's delivery, the mailing expense to deliver them is nil.

Improving the size and frequency of purchases is a job well suited to desktop-published materials. Building customer loyalty is another.

Virtually any service business can benefit from enhancing communication with current and potential clients. Often, these businesses are not a physical presence in customers' lives the way a grocery store or a gas station is, right there every time they drive down Main Street. You may only be a voice on the phone to your customers or an annual visitor who cleans the chimney or prepares the tax forms. By maintaining contact through written communication you leave a "paper trail" back to your door the next time your services are required, enhancing your share of mind and increasing customer loyalty.

You might want to create a leave-behind with valuable information that will encourage your customer to keep it around.

You might send out periodic mailings — a newsletter with seasonal tax tips from an accountant, for example, or a handy listing of airline phone numbers from a limousine service.

And when I say "communication" in discussing desktop publishing, I mean it to encompass the full range of written materials. That means company newsletters and advertising flyers, but don't stop your thinking there.

How about the forms you use?

And the reports you produce?

And the ads you run in newspapers and magazines?

And then there are specialty publishing jobs geared to particular businesses, like menus, programs for the audience at events your company organizes, and so on.

Desktop publishing makes business communication more economical and more timely. Use it skillfully as a strategic business tool and you may become a Goliath yourself.

YOUR OWN DESKTOP PUBLISHING BUSINESS?

There is a Great Divide in desktop publishing between using the technology to promote and expand your business and making desktop publishing *itself* your business. You can't do slapdash work in either case. But if your desktop publishing projects are limited to self-promotion activities, there is a lot more margin for error. Just the fact that you've moved from typewriter output to laser-printer output and set your text in columns with good-looking headlines could put you head-and-shoulders above the competition when it comes to making an impression on your own potential customers.

If you want to take on desktop publishing projects for someone else, though, you're in another ballpark. Now you're competing against other professionals, and you have to bring more than technology to the party. Desktop publishing offers cost and convenience advantages over traditional typesetting and page makeup techniques. But it still takes talent and skill to turn out good-looking publications, and those don't come off shelves labeled "hardware" or "software"; they have to be developed.

Casey Hill, a desktop publishing professional from Grand Blanc, Michigan, who also teaches the subject to budding page jockeys at local colleges, offers this caveat: "It seems like there are quite a few articles on starting a DTP [desktop publishing] business, and I think it is a bit troubling. For someone who has a good sense of design, and has done design or production work 'the old fashioned way' with traditional typesetters and equipment, the switch to DTP is a natural. But for people just looking around for a way to make some extra money with their computers, well…DTP takes a whole lot more work than just buying a program and putting up your 'in business' sign."

So much for rose-colored glasses! But I agree that there has been far too much written on this subject along the lines of great matchbook cover come-ons: Make Big Money Driving the Big Rigs! Buy a DTP Program and Earn $$$ the Easy Way! It's *never* that easy. But at the same time, people are doing it successfully.

Professional-Quality Work From a Basement Office

What makes the effort worthwhile, in my estimation, is the fact that the work you create using a personal computer *can* hold its own against traditional typesetting.

ACT Graphics is a case in point. John Cornicello and two partners started this Cranford, New Jersey, business in January 1990 in an apartment, and moved into the basement of one partner's new home a year later. Their software is pretty standard for a desktop publishing operation: *Microsoft Windows 3.0*, *Aldus PageMaker*, and

CorelDRAW running on two 386-based PC clones. The assignments they tackle with this setup are impressive, though, including typesetting for local printers, local ad agencies, and magazines. Where do three guys working out of a basement come off turning out pages for *Fitness Plus*, *Muscle Training*, *Oui*, and other publications?

The answer isn't hardware or software — it's smarts. One of the partners has thirty-five years' experience in conventional typesetting while John is the resident computer maven. The third partner is a salesman adept at "schmoozing with the clients."

"It's Just Me Running the Show"

A three-man business with decades of relevant experience between them is definitely a high-end success story. A more typical example comes from Susan Quinn in North Carolina.

"I run a DTP business called Infographix out of my home," Susan writes. "I do several different types of projects, including brochures, newsletters, logo design, ad design, flyers, and posters using a Mac II with a LaserWriter IINT. I am also a freelance magazine writer who does both medical journalism and writing for a publication of the Government & International Studies Department at the University of Carolina.

"I have found many of my clients through direct mail, newspaper ads, and word of mouth. Advertising is crucial. I advertise in a small weekly paper and sometimes in the business section of the daily paper. I have also taken out a good-size ad in the *Yellow Pages*. Another invaluable source of clients has been my local chamber of commerce, which is very helpful to small businesses.

"As far as tips go, the most important thing is to work hard and not settle for anything but your very best. I know that sounds trite, but the bottom line is that if you do poor-quality work, the word gets around, and no amount of advertising can cure that."

Parlaying Existing Skills Into Desktop Publishing Success

John Cornicello and his partners are professionals who were empowered to go it on their own by the availability of reasonably priced, powerful desktop publishing technology. Susan Quinn's experience is closer to my own — someone who starts out with expertise in one aspect of the publishing process (specifically, writing) and expands on that established skill to create a desktop publishing business.

Don Arnoldy in California is a graphic artist using a Mac-based system to turn out everything from 4-color posters to forms and technical documentation. He has fifteen years' experience in graphic arts, six with desktop publishing, and four as his own boss working from his home.

John Pantuso has a full-time job as director of publications for a national nonprofit organization, and a growing number of clients who use the DTP services he offers as a second business. "I'm not particularly interested (or gutsy enough) to cut myself loose from a good-paying fun job with decent benefits for going it alone in DTP land," he writes, "but I can nicely supplement my income and look forward to retiring and continuing to supplement my income with my DTP operation."

The Common Threads

We've covered a fairly diverse crop of desktop publishing businesses here. What do they all share?

First, they are all based on computer equipment that is fairly affordable. John Cornicello and his partners at ACT Graphics output final pages on a high-resolution imagesetter, which is not a purchase the average home-based businessperson would consider. But my clients get the same high-resolution output as John's, and you won't find an imagesetter stuffed into my small office or strapped budget; I have pages output for $3.50 to $7 (depending on the size of the job) each by an outside service bureau.

All of these DTP businesses were started by someone with some publishing skills. Can you start from scratch and become a professional desktop publisher? Sure, but it's easier if you start out with at least one aspect of this multifaceted undertaking under your belt.

If you're going to try making serious money at desktop publishing, you have to make a commitment to quality — perhaps even more quality than a particular client seems to demand. A satisfied customer is the beginning of a network of recommendations. Over the course of more than ten years on my own, that's become the only way I find new clients. Remember also that each successfully completed project adds another sample to show prospective clients.

Finally, you have to learn as much as you can and keep soaking up information like a sponge because this field changes rapidly. Read everything you can find on desktop publishing. Invest in a modem and check out the DTP-related areas on commercial on-line services and private bulletin boards. And learn by observing the wealth of professionally produced publications that cross your desk.

With the proliferation of computer/laser printer combinations, simply having the technological capability to turn out typeset pages is a pretty poor commodity to market. You have to sell smarts, and the more you learn, the more you're likely to earn.

Finding Those First Assignments

One of the most difficult hurdles in establishing a desktop publishing business (or any small business, for that matter) is finding those first paying assignments. Let's start by developing some criteria for identifying what makes a project suitable for desktop publishing newcomers.

Plays to Your Strengths

Are you a wiz with words? A top-notch illustrator? A designer whose work gives off sparks? Evaluate your special skills and look for projects that stress those abilities. For example, an excellent illustrator may be able to create a one-page flyer that captures the recipient's attention and delivers information about the product or service being promoted with a large, dramatic graphic and very few words.

Matches Your Existing Clients' Needs

Unless you are entering the business world for the first time, you probably have a number of established contacts. You may never have undertaken a communications-oriented project for them, but you still know them and, more important, they know you. That means you will at least have the opportunity to pitch to someone who doesn't regard you as a stranger.

Now evaluate the ways desktop publishing opens up new avenues to service those contacts' needs. That's the way I originally got into desktop publishing: taking on the production of a newsletter I had been hired to write. The client had an in-house art department with more work than the staff could handle. I offered an economical alternative. Voilà! I was in business.

Provides a Good Portfolio Piece

Samples sell. Designers call a really handsome project suitable for use in attracting additional clients a *portfolio piece.* As you begin to build your desktop publishing business, developing your sample portfolio is a major consideration.

Of course, you can always crank out desktop-published material for make-believe businesses to use as samples and probably should. But they won't have the same impact with potential clients as a real project you completed for a real client who paid you real money. And if the project made money for the client as well, then you have the ideal portfolio piece.

If you do have a success story, think about ways to use it effectively. Clearly you'll want to ask for a substantial number of printed samples. But consider taking this a step further. If the client's very happy, ask if you can have prospects call for a recommendation. Another useful tool for marketing yourself: a simple one-page letter from the client indicating satisfaction with your work.

Do you want to show off your skills by taking on a project for the local PTA, church group, or community theater? Setting aside for a moment the psychic satisfaction involved in doing pro bono work, is it good for business? Yes, *if* you get credit on the printed piece and that credit includes enough information for prospective clients to contact you directly. Frankly, I wouldn't place a lot of stock in building business this way, though I have anecdotal evidence that it works. However, this could be a great way to create a handsome portfolio piece, and you'll probably feel better about yourself for chipping in some time and effort.

Pays Well

Pricing is an extremely difficult issue. Virtually identical end products will be priced radically differently depending on the nature of the client. "Reasonable" prices vary based on geography too, and on the uniqueness of the service you're offering. If you have training in biochemistry, for example, you may be able to charge a significant premium for your specialized knowledge when undertaking a project for a pharmaceutical company. The same person undertaking a project of the same desktop publishing complexity will have to moderate fees substantially if the client is a company that runs children's birthday parties.

Start by deciding how much you need to make an hour. Include your own time, supplies, overhead for office space (even if you're working in a home office), and a bit more for wear and tear on your equipment. Then estimate the number of hours a project will take and multiply. Add a little if you think the client's used to spending money, subtract a bit if you think the client's pinching pennies but you really want the job (perhaps as a portfolio piece).

Then, present a bid for the job — *not* an hourly fee. I've been asked more than once to bid on jobs based on an hourly rate, but I don't like it. It's an inappropriate way to bill for creative work, when ideas may come quickly or slowly depending on the flight patterns of your personal muse. Besides, I'm folding a lot of overhead and downtime into the hour I use in calculating a bid, so my bid may sound high when judged on an hourly basis.

Fortunately, desktop publishers are often competing against businesses with higher overhead and larger staffs, so their bids often come in sounding extremely reasonable by comparison.

Represents Opportunity for Repeat Business

Some jobs are clearly one-shots. Some are one-shots that unexpectedly lead to further assignments. But that most desirable of assignments is the one that calls for new versions on a regular basis.

What kind of projects do I have in mind? How about preparing menus for a catering operation? It's certainly an elegant touch for the caterer to offer: a personalized menu for each client's affair. And while you can't charge a fortune for each rendition, even $50 a shot can come to an awful lot of money over the course of a year if you hook up with a busy caterer.

More ideas for repeat business: organizations with annual or semiannual membership directories; companies that produce sales literature for new products; and companies that use seasonal promotion strategies (holiday sales, for instance).

Some Ideas to Pursue

Desktop publishing calls for creativity not just in the execution of projects but in their original conception too. If you go to a potential client and say, "I have an idea that can help you make money," you'll get a better reception than "I can execute the ideas you come up with."

Think like a marketer. Look at businesses in your community and ask yourself, "What could I create in print that would help make money for that company?" Then approach the owner with your idea. Don't create the piece and walk in trying to sell it — you devalue your work by working "on spec." However, you might rustle up samples that *relate* to the concept you're selling without making it look too easy to undertake the project for the prospect's business.

I looked around my own local area for ideas I'd pursue if I were just starting out. Here's what I came up with.

Menus

I'm hot on menus as desktop publishing projects right now, partly because they can represent repeat business. But I also find they're an underutilized marketing resource for the food businesses in my area. A menu does a whole lot more than tell folks what's on the menu; menus communicate a tone, style, ambiance, and sense of expectation about the food. With the right menu, I can make each dish look as if it's worth two or three dollars more.

This is especially true for the take-out restaurants I patronize. Most of their menu designs are somewhere between mediocre and lousy. By adding some sophistication, an attractive organization, and a layout that doesn't look like the menus I remember from thirty years ago, I can turn that boring list of eats into an inviting sales document that would give the restaurant a competitive edge.

Flyers

Flyers work as business builders, especially for small businesses. We're talking lawn services, chimney cleaners, home-repair and improvement contractors, dog groomers, delivery services...the list goes on and on. Often, these one-sheet promotional pieces do triple

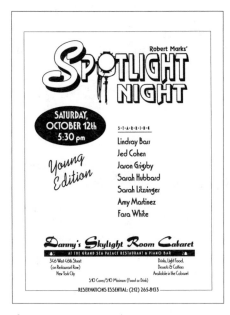

Robert Marks is a New York theatrical coach with a thriving side business in desktop publishing. He created this flyer to promote a showcase night for his students.

duty, serving as take-aways, postings on bulletin boards, and inexpensive mailing pieces.

I'd look first at some nearby businesses that are already using flyers for marketing but shortchanging themselves through poor copy and design. That way I wouldn't have to sell the concept of using flyers to those businesses, just prove that I can do it better.

I'd also look at businesses that could be selling themselves effectively through flyers but aren't. My first stop: an upscale bakery that opened in the area recently with truly extraordinary cakes and virtually no recognition in the community — they're too new and moved into a building that wasn't a bakery before. I could design some flyers to be inexpensively quick-printed and distributed door-to-door locally by the owner's kids. Project a high-class image in the copy and the design, include a $1-off coupon, and my services could be a superb investment for this fledgling business.

Résumés

Servicing job-seekers' needs for professional-looking résumés is a growth business around here. And while you can't charge a fortune for each résumé (I wouldn't want to ask more than $20 for the original ready to be reproduced), do ten of those a week and you've got a nice chunk of change each month.

The problem with desktop-published résumés as a business opportunity is that it's a little bit *too* easy. That translates into plenty of competition. I look at the bulletin board at my local college and find a dozen different offers for "typeset" résumés. Every quick-print shop in the area also offers résumé-preparation services. However, there are other, unexploited places where a résumés service could be effectively promoted.

I didn't find any ads for résumé-preparation services in my local weekly shopper's paper (they're called *Pennysavers* around here). I'd invest $20 in placing a classified ad there. I also checked the bulletin boards at all the local supermarkets but couldn't find a flyer promoting résumé-preparation services there either. It's worth a shot, but I wouldn't bet my mortgage money on making my mortgage money this way.

Collateral Materials

Many companies regularly use publications in their marketing programs. They often turn to ad agencies to produce them, although they aren't, strictly speaking, advertising projects. I'm talking about product brochures and flyers, price lists, press releases, public relations publications, instruction manuals, assembly directions, and more. These publications are often referred to as *collateral materials*. A good communicator with desktop publishing capabilities can compete effectively on both price and quality in this area. But it isn't always easy to get in the door.

I'd concentrate on getting some impressive samples together, even if they were for fictional companies. Then I'd go all out to create a slick printed package promoting my own services. How you sell *yourself* will tell a lot about how you will sell another company's goods and services.

Finally, with your self-promotional materials ready, you need somebody to solicit. There are directories in most local libraries put out by chambers of commerce and other sources that offer information about area businesses, often including executive names and titles. I'd look first for companies with products and services that match aspects of my personal educational experience and professional background. Then I'd widen my net to include companies that manufacture or import products (as opposed to services), since each change in product line entails new printed materials. I'd look for specific executives to contact; in a large company that might include the vice president of marketing, the executive in charge of corporate communications, and the employee benefits department (often involved in internal communication). For smaller companies, the routing is easier: Send it to the boss.

Before sending anything, I'd make a phone call to get the name of the appropriate individual (or confirm that the name I found in a directory is still correct). Without a specific name to target I'd hesitate to send my materials at all: Mailing to the "Marketing Department" is like mailing directly to a trash can.

The "whys" of desktop publishing along with some specific project ideas are discussed in Chapters 8 through 10. Right now let's turn our attention to the "hows" of desktop publishing, starting with the computer equipment you'll need to get the job done.

CHAPTER 2

What Hardware Do You Need?

Medical science continues its search for a Hardware Lust cure.

To the best of my knowledge, modern psychiatry has never chronicled the compulsion from which I suffer. But it's real, and I've got it bad. And though I have no documentary evidence to support my contention, I'm sure it afflicts millions of other computer users around the world.

Yes, I'm talking about…Hardware Lust!

The symptoms? Your eyes grow large when confronted with the latest and greatest the computer industry has to offer. You lose perspective. You think strange thoughts. "If the kids eat less and we give up cable TV, I can afford that new 600-megabyte hard drive." A really desperate sufferer might actually say something like that out loud.

And of course, there is the compulsive twitching of the fingers as you reach for your credit cards at the computer superstore.

There are cures for Hardware Lust. The most pleasant, I suppose, would be a big lottery win, allowing the poor sufferer to indulge the disease. The more common prescription, though, is a dose of Reality.

Don't look at computer advertisements for help on that score. In fact, "desktop publishing" is one of the most commonly offered excuses for buying the latest-greatest-most-expensive hardware on the market. It's tough to convince computer shoppers that they need state-of-the-art hardware to run a word processor or even a spreadsheet program. But when "desktop publishing" enters the picture, common wisdom (at least within the advertising community) says there's no end to what you should spend.

Here's your daily dose of Reality: You may very well be able to produce highly respectable desktop publishing projects on the computer system you already own. And if you can't, a fairly ordinary computer and a slightly-better-than-average printer are all you need to get up to speed without breaking the bank.

THE ESSENTIALS

What computer equipment do you really need to get involved in desktop publishing?
- A computer equipped with hard disk and a high-resolution monitor and video card
- A mouse or trackball, used for pointing at objects on the computer screen
- A printer that produces high-resolution output

What might you want to add to your desktop publishing hardware arsenal?
- A scanner for capturing images from printed sources
- A modem to connect your computer through the telephone line to outside resources

I'll tackle each of these equipment categories in turn, with advice tailored to three key considerations:

What You Absolutely Need

You will often find text on software boxes that lists "Minimum System Requirements." These are technically accurate (the software will run on the specified machine), but too often the word "run" is an exaggeration. "Crawl" or even "limp" might be more apt. When I suggest hardware you absolutely need, I mean equipment that keeps frustrating slow system performance within tolerable limits.

One of my primary concerns in suggesting minimum system requirements is to give you a benchmark against which to judge your existing equipment. It may not be the best desktop publishing system you could buy, or even adequate if your desktop publishing interests become substantial, but it may be good enough for starters.

What You Want

This is my specification for a reasonably powerful desktop publishing system — one that will move quickly through standard page-layout procedures, with some room for expansion if your needs increase. I'm also looking for ways to get you "the most bang for the buck," with enough power to accomplish serious work but without overkill or enough horsepower to impress your friends with your desktop "muscle machine." Keep in mind that this is a system tailored for the needs of an "average" business office, rather than a professional graphic design studio.

Hardware Lust

Give me a blank check and this is the equipment I'll spend it on. I won't devote a lot of attention to this category, since I'm sure most of you are as cost-conscious as I am. Some computer hardware "luxuries," though, are indisputably useful if you can afford them. It's worthwhile knowing about products that can save you time and effort, even if they aren't absolute necessities.

THE FIRST QUESTION: MAC OR PC?

Yes, we've all seen the news reports: IBM and Apple are bosom buddies now. They're going to work together to create computers and operating systems. They're going to transform personal computing. Their employees have stopped throwing rolls across the room at each other at computer industry luncheons.

But whatever the ultimate outcome of The Great Alliance, for the foreseeable future budding desktop publishers have a decision to make: Apple Macintosh or one of the myriad PC-compatible systems.

During the early years of desktop publishing, there was no need to make a decision. You went Macintosh. Thanks to Apple's LaserWriter printer and *Aldus PageMaker* page-layout software, the Macintosh system owned the desktop publishing market for years. You simply couldn't tackle the same publishing projects on a PC-compatible computer.

That situation has changed, though. Today the software and peripherals needed to produce first-rate documents on a PC-compatible are readily available. It is no longer mandatory that you switch to a Mac to become a desktop publisher.

Still, differences remain between the two competing standards. Here are the points of contention, in a nutshell.

Ease of Use

Macintosh is legendary for being easy to learn and easy to use. Three components contribute to this effect.

First is a Graphical User Interface (frequently shorthanded as GUI). That means the screen displays a close approximation of your final printed outcome, files on your disk are displayed on-screen as icons to make file management easier, and a pointing device (usually a mouse) is used to select items on the screen and manipulate them.

While Macintosh standard-bearers will quibble, you can find perfectly acceptable implementations of a GUI in desktop publishing programs for PC-compatible computers today.

The second component is standardization between programs. That is, different Macintosh programs will perform a given task in pretty much the same way whether you're running a word processor, or a spreadsheet, or a page-layout program, or whatever. Want to print something on a Mac? Go to the File menu and choose Print, or hold down the Command key and the letter "P" simultaneously.

The same level of standardization is only a dream on PC-compatibles. Even within the Microsoft Windows graphical environment, where programs look pretty much the same, the keystrokes needed to accomplish common tasks such as printing or deleting material vary widely.

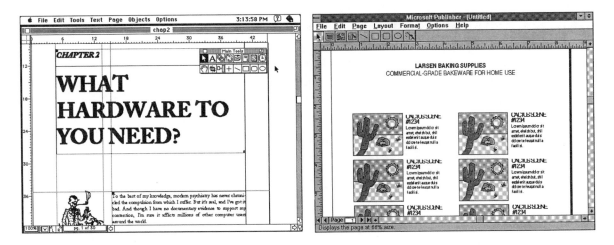

The Macintosh (shown at left running Personal Press, the program used to prepare this book), is the ease-of-use champ, but page layout software such as Microsoft Publisher (shown at right) brings a respectable graphical user interface to PC-compatible computers.

Finally, the ability to share information between programs contributes to the Macintosh ease of use. If I want to move a picture from a painting program to my page-layout program on a Macintosh, I can simply highlight the artwork, copy it to a temporary holding area in computer memory called the Clipboard, and paste it into the page layout. The same trick works within Microsoft Windows, and both the Macintosh operating system and Windows provide additional, more sophisticated ways of linking data between applications as well. However, if you're using a PC-compatible with non-Windows desktop publishing software, moving text and illustrations into your layout will be more time-consuming than it would be on a Macintosh. Make no mistake — it can be done, and it works fine. It just isn't as easy.

Widespread Acceptance

The computer system you choose locks you into a market segment. From then on, you will only be able to avail yourself of the computer peripherals, software programs, and outside services that support your chosen computer system.

Today both Macintosh and PC-compatible computer systems are

widely used for desktop publishing, at all levels of proficiency. Although the Macintosh is widely perceived as the machine of choice among graphic arts professionals, the total number of PC-compatible computers in use is roughly ten times the number of Macintosh computers. These two factors combine to ensure a complete and highly competitive selection of desktop publishing offerings from hardware manufacturers, software publishers, and other support services whether you're working with a PC-compatible or a Macintosh.

Price

The price situation has changed significantly in the past few years. Where once Macintosh computers were marketed as sports cars, the company now includes more reasonably priced family sedans in its product line. Even high-end Macintosh computers don't carry the same kind of price premium that once typified Apple products.

Even as Apple has moved to a more aggressive pricing strategy, though, the bottom has fallen out of pricing in the PC-compatible world. As I write this, you will still spend less for a PC-compatible computer than you would for a Macintosh of comparable speed and hardware features. And given the fact that Apple is the only source of Macintosh-compatible computers, while there are dozens of reputable vendors fighting for their share of the PC-compatible market, I don't expect that cost differential to disappear anytime soon.

Macintosh vs. PC-Compatible: The Bottom Line

So what are you going to do?

If you own a PC-compatible that's powerful enough for desktop publishing purposes, there's no compelling reason to switch to a Macintosh.

If you're shopping for a system, take a look at the machines in action and evaluate your personal price sensitivity. I still think the Macintosh is a superior desktop publishing computer today, but that margin is slimmer than ever before. Find a computer dealership where you can actually try out the machines. See if you agree with my assessment of the relative advantages and disadvantages, and see what kind of deal is available.

WHICH MODELS SHOULD YOU CONSIDER?

What You Absolutely Need

The original IBM PC and compatibles were based on an Intel 8086 microprocessor (or CPU). A machine of that class is really too slow for desktop publishing. However, the next step up, the so-called "AT-compatibles" based on the 80286 CPU will be adequate for basic needs.

On the Macintosh side, you can get away with one of the so-called "Compact Macs" for simple desktop publishing needs. These are the machines that incorporate a 9-inch monitor and the rest of the computer components in a single smallish box, including the older Macintosh Plus and SE and the current Classic line. The Classic II is significantly faster than the original Classic, and thus a significantly better choice.

The basic minimum memory requirement for a PC-compatible system is 1 megabyte, though you can squeak by with a 640K PC-compatible if that's what you've got. For a Macintosh, 2 megabytes is the practical minimum.

In addition to memory size, you'll have to decide on hard disk capacity. Although a few desktop publishing programs will run without a hard disk drive (i.e., from floppy disks), it isn't a practical solution. You need a hard disk. The absolute minimum size is 20 megabytes, though "standard equipment" on most computers sold today is 40 megabytes.

The Compact Macs combine computer circuitry and monitor in a single, relatively portable unit.

What You Want

The basic desirable PC-compatible computer for desktop publishing (and for most other purposes today) is based on the Intel 386SX microprocessor. These machines will give you the speed you need, let you run Microsoft Windows in its most capable form, and sell at a very competitive price.

Given the rapid decline in PC-compatible pricing, you may well find that the difference between a 386SX-based computer and its faster cousin, the 386DX (often simply called the 386) is inconsequential. If so, go with the faster model.

Although I said earlier that you can get away with a Compact

Mac, what you really want is a model with a separate computer and monitor components. That lets you use a larger monitor (a 12- or 13-inch screen is standard) and see more of the page you're working on at once. You can also expand the memory, improve the display system, and make other system upgrades more easily with these systems. In the Macintosh product line as of early 1992, the basic "what you want" machine is the Macintosh IIsi. It is powerful enough, expandable enough, and the price is reasonable.

At least 2 megabytes of random access memory (RAM) is desirable for a PC-compatible, 4 megabytes for a Macintosh.

Desktop publishing programs and files have voracious appetites for hard disk space. A 40-megabyte drive is the minimum desirable choice, and something in the 80-megabyte range is decidedly better without being horrendously more expensive.

The Macintosh II computer series offers greater speed and more expansion options than the Compact Macs.

Hardware Lust

The faster, the better.

Of course, that's always true with computers, but desktop publishing places fairly heavy demands on computer hardware. There are complex page elements to move and a highly detailed display to be recalculated and redrawn on screen whenever you make a change to a page layout.

What changes when you move up to a faster computer for desktop publishing is generally not the task that can be accomplished but how quickly it will happen. The faster the machine, the less time you will spend watching the computer catch up with your latest command.

Similarly, more memory is always welcome. A megabyte of memory now costs substantially less than $100 for most systems if you install it yourself, and there are plenty of ways extra memory will come in handy (assuming, of course, that your system isn't already loaded to capacity).

Many memory-hungry DTP programs run faster if there is more memory available.

If you are using an operating environment that lets you run several programs simultaneously (such as Windows 3.0 or DesqView on the PC and Multifinder or System 7.0 on the Mac), you'll be able to run more programs at once. Being able to jump instantly between your word processor, illustration program, and page layout software, for example, can be a tremendous time-saver.

And as programs with advanced linking capabilities become more prevalent, changes you make in one program can be automatically carried over into the other.

Similarly, there's no such thing as too much hard disk space. 100-megabyte drives are now commonplace, and should be adequate for serious desktop publishing users. However, 200- and even 300-megabyte drives are widely available and certainly desirable.

PUT YOUR MONEY WHERE YOUR MOUSE IS

Macintosh computers include a mouse as standard equipment. Some PC-compatibles are sold with a mouse included in the package, while it's an extra-cost option for others (that "extra cost" shouldn't come to more than $100).

One way or the other, you're going to need a mouse for desktop publishing. It's used for maneuvering through a graphical user environment, choosing commands from menus and files from lists or displays of icons. It's also used for positioning elements within a page layout, for drawing, and for playing *Tetris* when you just can't stand to do any more work for a while.

An alternative to the mouse that some desktop publishers adore is a trackball. That's basically a larger, stationary mouse turned upside down, so that instead of rolling the mouse around the table to move the ball inside, you just roll the ball itself with your fingertips. A trackball sits in one place, so you don't have to clear away any of your desktop clutter the way you would to find rolling space for a conventional mouse. On the other hand, a mouse puts the action button right under your fingertip, while a trackball requires a bit more contortion to hit the button. This one is purely a matter of personal taste, and the will-ingness to invest about $120 in a high-quality trackball.

MONITORING YOUR PROGRESS

Your computer's display system is vitally important to your productivity as a desktop publisher. The reason I'm covering the display system separately from the "basic box" computer elements (the system unit, memory, and hard disk drive) is that it's easier to upgrade than the other built-in components, and you have more qualitative as well as quantitative choices available.

There are two components in a computer display system: the monitor that shows you the picture, and a display adapter that processes the signals produced by the computer. Some computer systems come with built-in display adapters, while others have a slot inside the main unit available to hold the display adapter of your choice. Even a computer with built-in video capabilities can usually be upgraded to a higher display standard at a later date with the addition of a more powerful adapter and monitor.

What You Absolutely Need

You don't need a color display for basic desktop publishing (unless, of course, you're planning to undertake high-end color publishing projects, in which case you're going way beyond the basics).

And since it is relatively simple to upgrade most video systems, the display system may be the place to skimp when you first purchase a computer. In other words, if you're faced with the choice between buying a less powerful computer with a nicer display or a more powerful computer with only basic display capabilities, go for the latter. You can improve the display when you scrape a little money together. It's much more difficult, if not impossible, to improve the central processor unit in most computers.

The significant exception to this advice involves the compact Macintosh models with their built-in displays. Yes, you can improve the display systems of these machines by adding separate monitors and display adapters. No, you can't handle the upgrade job yourself (as you can with most other computers), and you'll pay a premium price, and you may experience software problems with what is essentially a kludged hardware solution. If you think you're likely to want a better display than the built-in 9-inch black-and-white monitor sometime down the road, try to avoid buying a compact Mac in the first place.

So what constitutes a practical minimum display system? A black-and-white monitor (ordinarily about 12 inches measured diagonally) and appropriate display adapter, whether built-in or added in on a card. If you already have a PC-compatible with either Hercules or

EGA standard display, you're fine. If you're buying a system now, there's no reason not to get the more up-to-date VGA standard display system, even if you'll be using a black-and-white monitor.

What You Want

The modular Macintosh computers come with built-in display capabilities that are perfectly adequate. PC users should be satisifed with a VGA standard display if that's what they own. If you're shopping for a new system now, so-called "super VGA" systems with improved resolution and the ability to display additional colors are now widely available for virtually the same price as ordinary VGA.

I assume you want a color display. Everybody wants a color display. I'm not entirely sure why people want to look at ordinary black-and-white pages on a color monitor...but then again, I can't understand how they let Ted Turner colorize *Casablanca*, so I guess I'm just behind the times.

Nevertheless, despite the fact that I know you're going to go out and buy a color display anyway, I'll propose two reasons why monochrome displays have a distinctive appeal. They cost less. And they are sharper, with only a single color to focus on a screen instead of combining three different colors.

Hardware Lust

Seeing more of your document on-screen at once is more than a cosmetic improvement: It lets you work faster and make better design decisions.

A display that shows you a full page at a time at approximately actual size (sometimes called a portrait monitor) lets you jump around the page by simply clicking your mouse in the desired spot. With a smaller monitor that displays only a piece of a page at a time, you'd have to tediously scroll to bring a new section of the page into view.

Seeing the entire page in one fell swoop also helps you identify graphic opportunities and problems, enabling you to create a more interesting and unified layout.

There are two sizes of large-screen monitors to consider: the single-page portrait monitor and the large, double-page screens that display an entire two-page spread at approximately actual size. You can also choose between monochrome or color systems in each size, though color in large-screen displays quickly becomes prohibitively expensive for anyone but a graphic arts professional.

In my own work I frequently use a PC-compatible with a single-page monochrome display. It's crisp and easy to read, gives me a good perspective on my work in progress, and can be found for about $1,000 today. An additional benefit of investing in a larger monitor for desktop publishing: You get to work on other applications on a larger screen as well. I find that word processing with the equivalent of a full 8½- by 11-inch sheet of paper on screen at once makes it easier to maintain a flow in my writing.

Before You Write That Letter

I see you now. Yes you, reaching for the keyboard of your Amiga or your Atari ST, ready to fire up the word processor and singe my ears with condemnation for not covering the desktop publishing capabilities of those systems in this book. Let me take a moment and try to save you a stamp.

I agree that you can produce handsome desktop-published documents on an Amiga or an Atari ST. And if you already own one and find yourself becoming interested in desktop publishing, you can certainly use it. But the sheer weight of numbers makes a Macintosh or a PC-compatible a better choice. Sticking with the two market-leading computer standards provides access to a wider selection of computer peripherals, application software, fonts, books, magazines, learning aids, and help from other users than you'll find within the Amiga or ST communities.

If there were some desktop publishing task that could be accomplished more effectively on an Amiga or an Atari, that would be a different story. But to the best of my knowledge, there isn't any.

Is it fair? Maybe not. But going with the standards is simply a more "no-sweat" decision than going with a less popular system.

PRINTERS DEMYSTIFIED

You're getting involved in desktop publishing to make an impression, right? You want to look professional. You don't want to look amateurish, or impoverished, or like you're not taking your own publication seriously. Agreed? Then you need at least 300-dot-per-inch (dpi) laser output for your printouts.

There are people out there devoting hours to writing, designing, and producing desktop-published documents who print out their work on dot-matrix or inkjet printers. That's sad and, what's worse, it's counterproductive. Blurry type that looks cheap and computer-produced is not going to impress anybody, and it's going to seriously undercut the impact of your message. In fact, a less-than-crisp print-out may be taken as proof that you're not the right person with whom to do business.

Even 300-dpi printing is not equivalent to the quality of professional typesetting, which typically has between 1,270 and 2,540 dots per inch. You can get that level of resolution for your own desktop-published documents by using an outside service bureau equipped with an imagesetter. We'll save that top-quality discussion for Chapter 10, though, since it isn't the way most people undertake day-to-day desktop publishing. For now, let's agree that 300 dpi is perfectly adequate for many projects, and anything less is not.

What You Absolutely Need

Any 300-dpi laser printer. Ideally the printer should at least be compatible with the popular Hewlett-Packard LaserJet models. That ensures that you won't have trouble making the printer work with virtually any software program on the market today. It also makes a decent selection of different typefaces available to you.

Laser printers are given speed ratings in terms of pages per minute. These ratings are fuzzy at best; the number of pages actually printed per minute depends on their content — all text, heavy graphics, lots of typefaces versus a single typeface, and so on.

The standard speed rating for most laser printers on the market used to be 8 pages per minute. Today there are many laser printers targeted toward individual users (versus networked office printers) that are rated at 4 to 6 pages per minute. I've worked with several of these and found them perfectly adequate for a single user. In fact, in many cases the speed ratio between a printer rated at 8 pages per minute and one rated 4 pages per minute is nowhere near 2 to 1 because of the idiosyncracies of the computer-printing process.

What You Want

What you want is a 300-dpi PostScript printer. That's the desktop publishing standard, and it's the most no-sweat solution available.

PostScript is a special-purpose programming language created by Adobe Systems that describes all aspects of a page — fonts, type styles and sizes, margins, graphic images, the works — for the computer printer. Some people actually write programs in Post-Script, but most desktop publishers use page layout and graphics programs that build the image we want on the screen and then automatically translate that image into PostScript code and send it to the printer.

One key advantage of PostScript is the freedom it provides for creating any type size you desire. Typefaces for the Hewlett-Packard LaserJet and other non-PostScript laser printers are bitmaps — dot-by-dot descriptions of each letter — stored on disk or in font cartridges. Every type size in every type style in this system requires a separate bit-mapped typeface file. The cost is high in both cash and disk space if you use a wide variety of bit-mapped typefaces. And you're up a creek if you suddenly need a type size you don't have.

PostScript fonts, on the other hand, are a set of instructions describing the shape of each individual letter. For example, the PostScript code for creating the letter "T" in, say, the Helvetica font, would tell the printer how to create the outline of the letter shape and fill in the middle. When you specify a type size, the printer draws the outline to that size and then creates the dot-by-dot representation ultimately needed to print the letter. PostScript fonts can also be rotated, manipulated, and shaded to create impressive special effects.

Some knowledgeable readers may be yelling at the page right about now. "But what about scalable font systems for non-Post-Script printers?" Relax, I'm getting there — but ideally that isn't where I want to be.

There are indeed a variety of software-based systems available for scaling typefaces to the size you want based on font outlines and outputting them on printers without PostScript. Some are better than others in terms of the amount of time they take and the quality of the type they produce. However, across the board, you will print more slowly using a software-based type scaling system than you would with PostScript printer hardware. You will be hard-pressed to find the variety and quality of typefaces available in the PostScript format duplicated in any other scalable font system (though Bitstream's Fontware and Facelift systems are undeniably good). In fact, Adobe has its own system for using PostScript fonts on non-PostScript printers (called Adobe Type Manager). But it still isn't as easy to use as genuine PostScript. And these type-scaling systems all leave a significant gap — graphic images.

PostScript graphics can be sized and manipulated freely, just as PostScript text can. If you draw a company logo at one angle using PostScript illustration software and later decide to tilt it, the image can be rotated in precisely specified increments without distortion. If that logo will be reproduced in a one-inch square, you can draw it much larger, then shrink it down. And if you have a small PostScript graphic that you want to enlarge, you can blow it up as much as you need and the resulting image will still have edges as crisp as the printer can produce.

The last important benefit of PostScript is called *device independence*. The same PostScript file you use to create a 300-dpi image on your laser printer can drive a professional Linotronic typesetting machine at 2,540 dpi and take advantage of the increased resolution.

You may have heard about TrueType, an alternative system to PostScript, championed by Apple and Microsoft. PostScript is owned by Adobe Systems, its developer. Anyone who wants to build PostScript into their equipment must pay Adobe a substantial royalty fee. Hence TrueType, an attempt to make PostScript and its license fee requirements obsolete.

The problem with TrueType is that PostScript works and has been widely accepted. The desktop publishing community, therefore, has greeted TrueType with substantial indifference. When choosing a printer, PostScript is still the no-sweat choice, and there's no indication that will change anytime soon.

Printers equipped with the new PostScript Level 2 will soon be commonplace, and there are enough improvements in the Level 2 enhancement to make it desirable. However, the improvements for black-and-white printing in PostScript Level 2 aren't dramatic enough to worry about if you already own a PostScript Level 1 printer or find one for sale at a good price.

Before moving on, let me add a suggestion for folks who already own LaserJet printers. Several plug-in cartridges are available to add PostScript (or PostScript workalike) capabilities to LaserJet printers. The price is a small fraction of the cost of a new printer, and the ones I've used work like a charm.

Hardware Lust

You can do better than 300 dpi in a desktop printer, and the improved resolution doesn't have to cost a fortune.

Look at printers equipped with Hewlett-Packard's resolution-enhancement technology. By varying the size and placement of the tiny dots, both text and illustration print out much more sharply than they do on an ordinary laser printer, which produces dots that are all the same size.

Apple has recently added similar refinements to its LaserWriter line with the introduction of the LaserWriter IIf (appropriate for single users) and IIg (for network installation) that improve type reproduction significantly and scanned-image reproduction dramatically. I was especially pleased to see that several older LaserWriter models can be upgraded to the new resolution standard very simply (you can handle the mechanics yourself) and at a reasonable price.

A few manufacturers carry resolution enhancement one step further. Through special-purpose printer design and/or custom controller boards that fit inside your computer, companies such as LaserMaster and NewGen provide output that's several degrees closer to professional typesetting quality and just as convenient as an ordinary desktop laser printer. These systems run several thousand dollars more than a 300-dpi laser printer, but that may be a reasonable investment if their high quality suits your business purposes.

SCANNERS

Scanners are cool.

I know it's a nontechnical, retro word, but there is something intrinsically "cool" about the ability to take an image from a piece of paper, suck it into your computer, and incorporate it in a report, proposal, newsletter or brochure, a piece of correspondence, a database file — or to fax the scanned image anywhere in the world with a fax modem.

And right now, scanners are hot. Inexpensive hand-held scanners have become serious graphic input tools. At the same time, prices for full-size flatbed scanners are tumbling, and features formerly found only on top-of-the-line models are now available in mid-priced units. Grayscale and even color scanning are no longer the exclusive domain of graphic arts professionals. And as we continue to move en masse from computers that comfortably handle only words and numbers to graphically capable systems that make illustrated documents easy to prepare, the desirability of owning an image scanner grows accordingly.

How Will a Scanner Help You?

Based on advertising and salesperson enthusiasm, it's easy to overestimate the desktop publishing capability of a scanner.

It *is* possible today to scan photographs (even color photographs) with a desktop computer and scanner and achieve magazine-quality printed reproduction. However, it is not a procedure I'd recommend for "no-sweat" desktop publishers. It involves outputting your files on imagesetter equipment directly to film, and can be both technically demanding and unnecessarily expensive. For most projects traditional photographic printing procedures are considerably simpler and cheaper than trying to scan your own photos for printed reproduction today.

There are plenty of projects where decent but imperfect photographic reproduction is good enough, though. A report or proposal, for example, does not require the same high-quality reproduction standards as a professionally printed brochure. Today's scanners will consistently produce a decent result when teamed with a 300-dpi laser printer. And when used with one of the resolution-enhanced models mentioned earlier, the output is impressive.

Where most scanners earn their keep in a desktop publishing environment, though, is in scanning photographs for positioning purposes and scanning line art for final reproduction.

Scanned photographs are unbeatable as working images. When you import a scanned image into your page layout, you can fine-tune cropping, sizing, and overall layout to your heart's content.

One of the wonderful aspects of desktop publishing is the ease and speed with which you can try out different design ideas.

Desktop publishing software lets you tinker with typography until it looks right. By adding a scanner to your system you can experiment with the size and placement of illustrations in the same way.

Including sized photo scans on a page lets you see exactly where type will fall. I find this indispensable when creating layouts in which type is wrapped around a graphic. Without an image on-screen, preparing this kind of layout is painfully tedious. With a scanned image in place, it's quick and easy.

Plus, when a project requires client approval, it's easy for me to present complete laser-printed output that provides an acceptable rendition of the final publication using carefully sized scans positioned where photographs will eventually fit.

The scanned, working images of photographs serve as tools for the print shop as well. Publishers and advertising agencies often paste down photostats (photographic prints prepared at a specified size) or sized photocopies to indicate the position and cropping of illustrations for the commercial printer to follow. These are marked *For Position Only* (FPO). The print shop substitutes correctly sized film versions of the photos when preparing for printing.

The cost of photostats and the time spent pasting in FPO images can both add up quickly. A scanned image is a perfect alternative.

Reproducing line art illustrations is another strong suit for scanners. A line art illustration is composed of lines and areas of a single solid color, as opposed to illustrations created with many shades and tints. Scanners do an excellent job capturing line art, which can then be directly incorporated in your page layout and printed out in position along with the type.

Before shopping for a scanner for your desktop publishing system, you should understand the two key factors used in categorizing scanners: size (flatbed versus hand-held) and image type (black and white, grayscale, and color).

Flatbed Scanners

A flatbed scanner works in much the same way as a photocopier: You place the original on a flat sheet of glass and a light-sensitive bar scans beneath it. A copier transfers the scanned information immediately to a hard-copy image; a scanner saves the information as a computer file.

Flatbed models can scan full 8½- by 11-inch sheets, and some models can also handle 14-inch legal-size originals. This is important both for large illustrations and for optical character recognition (OCR), the technology that allows you to scan in a printed page and have software "read" the printed words into a text file.

Since the flatbed's scanning mechanism is pulled across the image by a motor, the movement is precise and there is little chance of image distortion. And if you get into multi-page scanning projects (common in OCR applications), you can add a document feeder that will feed a stack of originals automatically.

However, flatbed scanners take up a significant chunk of valuable desktop real estate — most are over a foot wide and nearly 2 feet long. They are also expensive when compared to hand-held scanners: about three times the price for models with similar grayscale or color capabilities.

Hand-Held Scanners

Hand-held scanners have distinct limitations when compared to flatbed models. The size of the images you want to scan is clearly the most pressing concern. Most hand-helds are 4 inches wide, and the width of the image scanned is effectively limited by the width of the scanner. Some models come with software that allows you to "stitch" two separate passes together to create a full-width document scan, but this is inevitably time-consuming, often inaccurate, and best used by those who only occasionally need a wider scan.

There's also a certain level of manual dexterity required to use a hand-held scanner effectively. You are the motor here, and if your hand veers a little to the left or right, the resulting scan will have a psychedelic ripple effect that probably wasn't your intention. Some hand-held models are easier to guide than others, but the flatbeds still hold a decided edge when it comes to precision scanning (especially important if your original includes lots of straight lines).

Optical character recognition software that offers respectable text-recognition accuracy levels using hand-held scanners is available, but the inherent size limitation of the equipment makes these models a distinct second choice for automated text entry.

On the other hand, a good hand-held scanner is an excellent value. If you stick to relatively small originals and use the equipment properly, you can often achieve results indistinguishable from those obtained with a flatbed scanner, at a fraction of the price. And instead of finding a permanent desktop berth for a full-size flatbed, a hand-held scanner can rest in a few spare inches of space, or even be stowed away in a drawer between uses.

Black-and-White, Grayscale, and Color Scanners

Both hand-held and flatbed scanners come in three varieties. The simplest, least expensive versions record images only in terms of black dots and white dots. This is perfectly adequate in some cases. A line drawing, cartoon, or text document only has black and white in the first place, so there is no good reason to use a more elaborate scanning technology to capture the image.

The challenge becomes more complex when we want to scan continuous-tone originals. These are images that contain shades of gray or color in addition to black and white.

Take an original black-and-white photograph as an example. The name itself is inaccurate, since that "black-and-white" photo is actually composed of a multitude of gray shades and very little that is pure white or pure black. A scanner with only black-and-white capability, though, must translate those gray areas into patterns of black and white dots that look kind of gray when they're reproduced on paper.

A grayscale scanner, on the other hand, will record a number in its scanned image file that corresponds to a particular level of grayness. The ability to distinguish 256 shades of gray is the accepted standard currently — a far cry from simple black and white. Keep in mind, though, that it's also a far cry from the level of detail a standard desktop laser printer can effectively reproduce. For practical purposes, a 300-dpi laser printer is limited to reproducing about 16 shades of gray while retaining an acceptable level of image detail. In order to make use of the full grayscale scanning capabilities of today's scanners, you have to output the file on high-resolution imagesetting equipment.

There is another significant advantage to grayscale scanning — the opportunity to edit the captured image. With software either supplied with the scanner or purchased separately, a grayscale image can be resized significantly and maintain its sharpness. You can also enhance the image in important ways, such as increasing sharpness or manipulating image brightness and contrast, and retouch the image to eliminate imperfections or add highlights.

Color image scanning is conceptually similar to grayscale scanning, except that instead of recording shades of gray, the resulting file contains information corresponding to shades of color. As you might expect, the level of complexity grows astronomically when you leap from gray to what Disney so aptly called "the wonderful world of color." A 24-bit color scanner (such as the Hewlett-Packard Scanjet IIc) is capable of distinguishing over 16 million colors, and even a more modest color hand scanner (such as the Mouse Systems PC PageBrush/Color) can capture 4,096 shades.

The tricky question becomes: What are you going to do with that color once you've captured it? Our ability to scan a color image is currently a generation ahead of our ability to display or reproduce it.

There are, in fact, so-called "true color" graphics adapter/monitor combinations that do a credible job of displaying complex color images realistically on screen, but they are priced beyond the reach of those whose business applications aren't dependent on color-image manipulation. Most of us will view the results of our color scans on a more modestly priced display system. And if we have a color output device at all, it is probably better suited to computer-generated color documents such as graphs and line art than complex scanned full-color images.

Color for on-screen presentations? An excellent reason to purchase a color scanner. Even at VGA resolution, full-color scanned graphics make a good impression. And the same goes for adding some sizzle to reports and proposals where there is a logical reason to include color samples (preliminary product design sketches, for example). When it comes to applications where precise color reproduction is critical, though, I'm still wary. Chief among these applications is scanning color originals to incorporate in desktop publishing projects. Can it be done now? Absolutely. Is the process technically smooth and economically attractive enough for most desktop publishers to jump in now? I don't think so.

Still, in contemplating a scanner purchase today, I'll put on my Official Buck Rogers Futurevision Specs (standard issue to all computer journalists) and gaze into the near-term future. I see color reproduction and display technology improving in quality and price.

Scanning and image editing becomes "smarter" about making image optimization decisions, and multimedia applications become increasingly prevalent and important. In this scenario the ability to scan color images rapidly moves center stage. And since you probably won't want to replace your new scanner two years from now, I'd seriously consider making the investment in color scanning today.

However, don't sacrifice monochrome quality for the sake of color. I need grayscale scanning capability, now and for the foreseeable future, and I strongly suspect you do too. Some color scanners offer true grayscale as well as color scanning. Others fudge the issue, using software to create grayscale files from color-scanned information, which produces a less accurate image than real grayscale scanning. Caveat emptor!

What You Absolutely Need

There is no question that you can be a perfectly competent desktop publisher without owning a scanner. However, if you feel your projects justify the expense, here are some quick guidelines.

A simple black-and-white scanner will capture images of sufficient quality to be used for line art reproduction and as fairly crude photographic placeholders. If you are working with fairly small originals, a hand-held scanner should do the trick.

What You Want

Grayscale capability is extremely useful and doesn't add much to the cost of a scanner in today's market. The key advantage is the ability to edit and resize the scanned image with far more latitude than you have with a simpler black-and-white scan.

Unless your originals will consistently be less than 4 inches wide, a flatbed scanner is certainly more practical than a hand-held model. However, in terms of image quality, I have achieved excellent results with grayscale hand-held scanners, and they are priced to sell.

Hardware Lust

A color flatbed scanner with full grayscale capability. The Hewlett-Packard ScanJet IIc is the trendsetter at this writing, with top-notch quality and a very competitive price. "Competitive" is the key word here, though. Within the next year or two, I'll be very surprised if scanners with color/grayscale capabilities don't become the established standard equipment on the marketplace. As that occurs, prices are bound to drop a notch or two.

MODEMS

Modems are the gizmos that let you attach your computer to your phone line and connect with another modem-equipped telephone. What does that have to do with desktop publishing? Quite a bit, if you play your cards right.

There is a very active and growing community of desktop publishers who share information and resources (such as typefaces and illustrations) through commercial on-line information services (including CompuServe, Prodigy, and America Online) and hundreds of private computer bulletin board services across the country.

But you need a modem to access these resources, so here's a quick guide to help you find a model with the right price/performance profile.

What You Absolutely Need

You can sample computer telecommunications using just about any modem you can get your hands on, but if it's too slow or too difficult to operate, you won't get a true sense of the advantages the process provides. I'd rather skip directly to....

What You Want

A Hayes-compatible 2400-baud modem.

Hayes-compatible simply means that the modem adheres to a set of widely accepted industry standards. Most modems on the shelf today are Hayes-compatible, but it's always worth asking.

2400-baud is a speed rating. As you might expect, larger numbers mean faster communication, and faster is better. You might still find some 1200-baud or even 300-baud modems for sale (perhaps as used equipment), but 2400-baud speed is both the minimum practical choice and the accepted standard today. The discounted price for a

2400-baud modem from a reputable manufacturer is in the $100 to $150 range.

You'll also need telecommunications software to control the modem. Some modems include a telecommunications program with your hardware purchase. Often you'll find that a simple telecommunications program is perfectly adequate. Windows 3.0 owners are in luck on that score, since the *Terminal* accessory program provided with Windows is fine for beginners and may provide all the telecommunications capability you'll ever need. If you do have to buy software, you'll find good choices such as *Procomm Plus 2.0* for PC compatibles and *Smartcom* for the Macintosh selling for less than $100 at discount.

Hardware Lust

Modems operating at 9600 baud are rapidly gaining acceptance, and prices are dropping dramatically. The rest of the telecommunications world hasn't quite caught up with 9600 baud yet. Many bulletin boards and commercial information services still operate at 2400 baud. A 9600-baud modem will work perfectly well at lower speeds, though, and it won't be long before high-speed telecommunications becomes the prevalent standard. Check the price difference before making the 2400-baud versus 9600-baud decision.

CHAPTER 3

What Software Do You Need?

I used to turn up my nose at so-called low-end or midrange desktop publishing programs. They might be fine for the high school French club newsletter, but for business communication? With poor laser printer support, no hyphenation, time-consuming manual layout techniques, and an overall lack of polish and precision, I just couldn't take them seriously.

My standards haven't budged, but the quality of midrange page-layout software certainly has. The best of the current generation has obliterated my list of objections. What's more, while developers of high-end professional page-layout programs have largely concentrated their recent efforts on four-color process printing esoterica, the midrange folks have identified a host of real-world needs and filled them, often with considerable elegance, and at prices from one-quarter to one-third those of the high-end software.

You can produce really first-rate publications with these programs: flyers, newsletters, brochures, catalogs — you name it. It won't take you long to learn how, and it won't cost an arm and a leg. That sounds like a pretty good working definition of "great software" in my book.

A DIVERSE GROUP OF MIDRANGE PROGRAMS

There is an impressive array of midrange page-layout programs available today for both IBM-compatible and Macintosh computers, and more are on the way. Though they all fit comfortably under the "midrange" banner, these programs make up a highly varied group. No two have the same combination of strengths and weaknesses, and each has a distinctive personality.

I feel it's important to review several individual programs in this book, to give you a sense of the "state of the art" in midrange page-layout software and provide some guidance when shopping for this type of software. However, keep in mind that programs change over time, as publishers release new versions of their pride and joy. Sometimes the programs improve in significant ways. Sometimes they just sort of mutate into something different from the original but not necessarily more appealing. In either case, to be an informed consumer you'll need to understand the elements that will help you to distinguish between the different programs on the market. That way you can evaluate new programs that hit the shelves and the "improved" versions of the programs listed in this chapter.

We can group our evaluation criteria into five areas: ease of use, text handling, graphic capabilities, printer and font support, and file format compatibility.

Ease of Use

The central promise of midrange programs is that people without publication-production training can build attractive documents. Coming through on this promise entails a wide range of issues, from the basic organization and design of the program to the manuals provided and the availability and quality of technical support.

An area of special interest is the supply and implementation of templates. A template is a "canned" page design — a fill-in-the-

Microsoft Publisher offers a special kind of template automation. Using the program's PageWizards, you answer a series of design questions and the program custom-crafts a layout to your specifications.

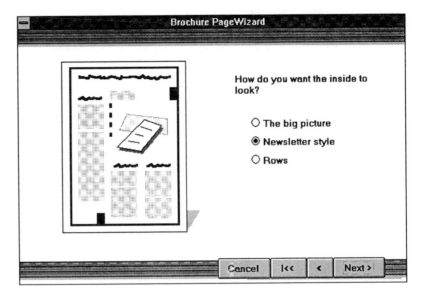

blanks document that supplies type specifications, illustration positioning, and graphic flourishes, inviting the user to place the actual text and illustrations and voilà! Instant publication! Often, when different versions of a publication will be created over time (issues of a newsletter, for example, or a series of flyers announcing special offers over the course of a year), the best strategy is to start off with a template and customize it to suit the individual project. In evaluating midrange desktop publishing software, we should consider both the templates supplied with the program, and any special features that make working with templates faster and easier. (We'll look more closely at templates in Chapter 7.)

Master pages are another time-saving feature. Instead of repeatedly placing text or graphic elements, such as page numbers, that should appear on all (or nearly all) of the pages of your publication, you can place them on a master page to include them automatically throughout. Ideally, you should have separate master pages for left- and right-hand pages.

Text Handling

There are two facets to DTP text handling — the placement of text blocks on the page and the features ordinarily associated with word processing that help us edit and proofread our writing.

The basic strategy for placing text on a page is fairly similar from

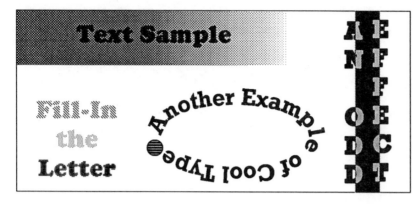

These fancy text treatments were created using the capabilities built into the Avagio page-layout program.

program to program, but the specific techniques used to implement that strategy can vary widely. For any text that will run longer than a single block or page, you have to link the separate text sections into a connected series. This can be accomplished as easily as a click here and a click there, but a few of the programs make the process far more complicated to no advantage.

Most of the programs reviewed here have autoflow capabilities to speed up placement of lengthy texts. With autoflow, if a story is too long to fit in a single page or text block, the program will automatically create additional pages to hold the remainder.

The way programs handle the interaction between text and

Find & Replace

Find:

Replace With:

Text Settings

Settings for: ● Find ○ Replace

Font: [Any] ☒ Any Style ☐ Plain

Size: [Any] [12] pts ☐ **Bold** ☐ Shadow
☐ *Italic* ☐ Condense

Style Name: [None] ☐ Underline ☐ Extend
☐ Outline ☐ Small Caps

Search Options

Search in: [This story] ☐ Words only

☒ Start from beginning ☒ Match case [Done]

[Find Next] [Replace, then find] [Replace All] [Replace]

Personal Press offers extensive search-and-replace capabilities, making it simple to change the wording or the formatting of your text automatically.

The powerful style sheet capabilities of Publish It! for PC-compatibles allows you to designate justification, font and size, tab settings, and more for selected text with a single menu selection.

```
┌─────────────────────────────────────────────┐
│        ┌───────────────────────────┐         │
│        │  PARAGRAPH STYLE for SUBHEAD │        │
│        └───────────────────────────┘         │
│                                              │
│                        ┌──────────────────┐  │
│                        │ Justification... │  │
│                        │ Font & size...   │  │
│   Paragraph format     │ Dimensions...    │  │
│                        │ Set tabs...      │  │
│                        │ Word spacing...  │  │
│                        ├──────────────────┤  │
│                        │ New style...     │  │
│   Other paragraph commands │ Delete style...  │  │
│                        │ Function key...  │  │
│                        └──────────────────┘  │
└─────────────────────────────────────────────┘
```

graphic elements on the page varies also, most notably in the program's ability to fit text around the edges of an illustration. Some programs can only handle rectangular graphics, while others can fit text around the edges of an irregularly shaped graphic. It isn't a design effect you're likely to use every day, but it's a useful capability to have on tap when a layout calls for it.

Additional graphically oriented text capabilities include the ability to rotate text at an angle and to create fancy display type effects. In fact, some of these programs let you distort, manipulate, and arrange type to create flashy, eye-catching type treatments worthy of a professional magazine publisher.

On the more mundane get-the-words-right side, a spellchecker and a thesaurus have become highly touted features in this product category (though you are likely to need them more in your word processor, while actually writing the text, than in your page-layout program). On the other hand, a robust search-and-replace capability is a tremendous time-saver. In the best implementations of search-and-replace you can not only look for strings of letters, but for the typefaces and typestyles they will be printed in as well. That's mighty useful if, halfway through a project, you decide to change the way the name of the product is presented from Gunko to GUNKO.

On the subject of typefaces (and sizes and styles, for that matter), the way you specify these type characteristics is a major point of differentiation among programs. The feature that lets you streamline the process is called a *style sheet*.

Say you want all of your subheads to be set in 14-point Palatino Bold, centered over the text column, with a blank space above each one. With a style sheet, you define a style containing that information and give it a label. Then, whenever you encounter a subhead, you just assign it a style in one step, instead of applying each type characteristic individually.

Ideally, styles should remain "live" while you work with a document. That is, if you change the definition of a style, all of the text you've formatted with that style name should change to match the revised definition. In midrange desktop publishing that's not always the case. Some programs offer a one-way style capability: they'll format the text to match your style specification but won't update text you've already formatted if you change the style later. It's better than no style sheet capability at all, but much less flexible than a "live" style sheet.

Finally, one potentially useful text-handling capability that often gets overshadowed by flashier features is the ability to export text from the page-layout program in a format that a word processor can read. You're unlikely to write lengthy pieces of text in your page-layout software, but often you'll make significant changes as you work with the text on the page. What happens if you need the same text in a word-processing file? Without text export capability, you're stuck making the changes manually, which is as error-prone as it is tedious.

Graphics Capabilities

There are certain common graphic elements you need to be able to create within your page-layout program. You should be able to draw lines and boxes, ideally with a high degree of flexibility in the weight and style of the lines involved. You should also be able to apply different levels of background shading to the boxes or other shapes you create in the program.

Many of the midrange DTP programs covered here go far beyond simply drawing lines and shapes, adding the ability to create drawings or edit graphics from other sources. Sometimes these capabilities take the form of fairly full-featured painting and drawing programs incorporated into the page-layout software — not a bad deal if you're looking for an all-in-one solution.

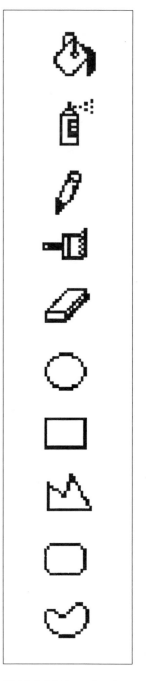

Publish It! Easy *for the* Macintosh *provides extensive built-in graphics tools.*

Printer and Font Support

This is much more of an issue with PC-based desktop publishing programs than with the Macintosh. That's because the Macintosh operating system takes care of all the potentially messy font handling housekeeping for Mac applications. On the PC, though, the operating system takes an every-application-for-itself attitude, making font handling a significant issue both for software publishers and software users.

One popular solution to this problem is Microsoft Windows, which handles printer and font support for Windows-based software. So far, the major player in midrange Windows-based desktop publishing is *Microsoft Publisher*. (The high-end desktop publishing programs are also well represented in the Windows environment, with both *Aldus PageMaker* and *Ventura Publisher*.

Two of the programs covered here rely on a graphical environment from Digital Research called GEM. Although GEM doesn't have the popularity of Windows, it is similar in its role as mediator between user and printer, and is well supported by third-party typeface vendors. The other two PC programs reviewed here go it alone, with mixed results.

In evaluating printer and font support, we have to look at both the range of printers the program can use and the variety of available typefaces. Some of these programs come complete with their own selection of typefaces. If your design demands are relatively modest, that may be all you'll ever need.

File Format Compatibility

Page-layout software is where your publication all comes together, but it usually isn't where each of the individual elements that make up the pages is created. Most of us use word processors for creating text and illustration programs, clip-art disks, or image scanning software for graphics. These varied sources produce files in a wide array of formats — and the more omnivorous your page-layout program is in accepting diverse formats, the better.

Of course, you can always save a word-processing document as a plain vanilla ASCII text file and import that into your page-layout software, but you lose formatting information (such as boldface and italicization), which you then have to re-create in your page layout program. If the page-layout program is set up to accept your word processor's native format, it will retain the formatting you've already created and save several steps.

On the graphics side, there are a number of standard formats, each supported by a variety of illustration programs. Problems arise when your page-layout program doesn't handle files designed for laser-printer resolution well, leading to size distortion or poor printing results. You also want to be sure that the program can accept object-oriented drawings such as EPSF (Encapsulated PostScript Files) on both PC-compatibles and the Macintosh. Object-oriented drawings can be enlarged or shrunk down freely, and will always print at the full resolution of your system printer, without distortion.

Another area of differentiation comes up when dealing with files created using an image scanner. A scanned image can be saved in two basic ways: as a picture composed of a pattern of black-and-white dots or in a grayscale format that stores more detailed information about the image. Grayscale scans are easier to work with when it comes to reducing or enlarging the image within a page-layout program. The catch is that the software has to support grayscale scans, and many midrange page-layout programs don't. You'll still be able to use a scanned image saved in one of the less flexible formats, but if scanning is going to be a regular part of your publishing activities, go with grayscale.

WHAT AREN'T YOU GETTING?

We're talking about programs here that are significantly less expensive than the more widely publicized, high-end choices (*PageMaker*, *Ventura Publisher*, and *Quark XPress*, for example). You must be giving up something, right?

Well, the answer to that is a definite "maybe." You're not giving up anything if what's missing is a program capability you would never use anyway. And for many users that's precisely the case for several features found in premium-priced page-layout programs.

For instance, you won't find automatic table of contents or index preparation included in midrange programs. Full-color separations? Nope, though it's going to be a while till I'm ready to switch from tried-and-true traditional methods to desktop color photographic publishing when I need to include a full-color photo in my publications anyway.

The high-end programs do include some text handling niceties that I miss when using midrange software. For example, control over automatic hyphenation and page breaks is more precise in high-end software. I can tell *Ventura Publisher* that I don't want more than two lines in a row to end in hyphens and the program will proceed accordingly. Only *Personal Press* among the midrange programs provides this level of control. Similarly, *Ventura Publisher* will eliminate widows and orphans (unsightly single or partial lines left hanging at the beginning or end of a text column). High-end programs also provide a level of precision down to a minute fraction of an inch that's lacking in the midrange programs, but the times when that level of precision is needed are few and far between.

I could go on with a list of relatively technical capabilities and some genuinely timesaving types of automation that are lacking in midrange programs. More important than what's lost by choosing to go the midrange route, though, is what's gained. And that can be substantial.

At an elementary level, there are differences in the computer hardware required to run the software effectively. Midrange programs consume a relatively modest amount of hard-disk space and run happily in far less memory and with slower processors than their high-end cousins. Pity the poor DTP newcomer who tries to run *PageMaker 4* on the Macintosh Classic that was so invitingly inexpensive. Sure, the program will run — but it's more of a crawling, herky-jerky motion than an actual "run." Far better to use a *Publish It! Easy* that is designed to work on a more modest hardware platform.

There is also an undeniable appeal to a K.I.S.S. (Keep It Simple, Stupid) design philosophy. Instead of a mammoth array of menus and dialog boxes that heap complexity on top of confusion, these programs offer a direct approach. You want two columns of text with a headline across the top and a picture at the bottom, and you want it to look good coming out of your laser printer. Fine. Spend a few minutes with one of these programs and you've got it. And as your design sophistication grows, the right program from this selection will give you the flexibility you need to fully indulge your creative urges.

MIDRANGE DESKTOP PUBLISHING BUYER'S GUIDE

To help you grasp the significance of the differences between various desktop publishing programs, I've created a sample flyer for a fictional business and attempted to reproduce it using each of the programs evaluated here.

Anatomy of an Example

I recently added a puppy to our home office (that's Bonnie at the lower right of the flyer on page 51, making her modeling debut). When we visited the veterinarian's office there were a number of brochures and flyers arrayed on a side table, including several from national companies and a few from local dog training and pet supply establishments. Nothing from any of the groom-your-dog-at-your-home businesses that exist in my area, though. Hence Groom Service, an imaginary but plausible home-based business, was born.

My design goal in creating the flyer (beyond exploring the capabilities of the desktop publishing programs under consideration) was achieving a certain sense of class and reliability — after all, Groom Service expects you to trust it with a valued member of the family. I needed a substantial block of body text and wanted to include a coupon to spur first-time customers. Finally, the phone number had to stand out, since that's the only way customers are going to find John and Mary Smith.

In trying to duplicate this design using each of the midrange desktop publishing programs, I fudged as little as possible. If I couldn't re-create part of the design from within the program, I substituted something close (for typefaces, for example) or left it out entirely. It's worth noting, though, that I could have used additional software to fill in the blanks in some cases. For instance, the "INTRODUCING" type block could have been created in a drawing program and imported as a graphic. But that would have been cheating.

Another key point to keep in mind is my output device, a PostScript printer, using PostScript fonts. You don't need a PostScript printer for desktop publishing. However, it is the best tool for the job, not least of all because PostScript has become a de facto desktop publishing standard, ensuring plenty of support in

❶ *This little banner requires two page-layout capabilities — reversing white text out of a black background, and rotating type. To get the black background shape, I created a rectangle, rotated it 45°, then placed solid white rectangles along the outer margin to mask off the excess, creating outside edges that run parallel with the live page area.*

❷ *Our Groom Service waiter started out as an EPSF clip-art file from T/Maker's Clickart collection. The only alteration I made was to stretch the tray horizontally (using CorelDRAW). To save time I added the "Groom Service" text in CorelDRAW (on the PC) and Adobe Illustrator (on the Mac), set in Adobe's Caslon Openface, and saved it as part of the image in EPSF format.*

❸ *The enlarged letter "J" is a graphic device called a drop cap. It's created in its own snug-fitting frame and placed so the body text wraps around the rectangular boundary.*

❹ *The paw print started out as clip art too (from Arts & Letters Editor this time). I saved it as a 300-dpi PCX format file for the PC, and a 300-dpi PICT file for the Mac. Note the way the body text follows the shape of the illustration.*

❺ *I drew a rectangle, added a border and filled it with a medium-gray tone, then centered a smaller rectangle with a thin black border and white fill inside it to hold the body text. Notice the thick-thin double line on the outer border. It's called a scotch rule and adds an elegant touch for boxes or line elements on a page.*

❻ *Body text is set in the Adobe Caslon typeface, regular and bold, in two justified columns with 1.5 picas in*

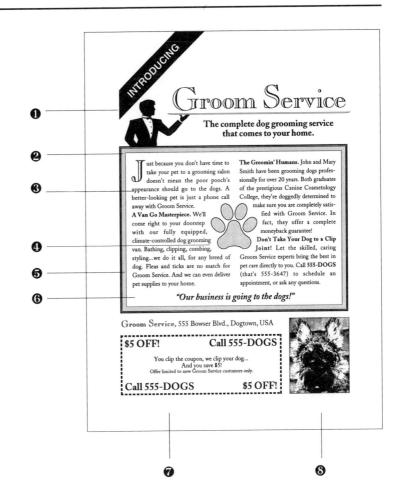

between. While you shouldn't expect each program to break the text lines at exactly the same spot, you should look for attractive horizontal text spacing and correct hyphenation.

❼ *Another rectangle drawn within the page-layout program, this time with a dotted-line border appropriate for a coupon.*

❽ *My initial scan of Bonnie's picture was a grayscale image*

created using Logitech's Scanman 256 hand-held scanner and enhanced with its Ansel image-editing software. I soon discovered, however, that the ability to accept a grayscale image was the exception rather than the rule among midrange DTP programs so I scanned the image again, this time in straight black and white, at the actual size I would be using. Both scanned images were saved in TIFF format files (which can accommodate both black-and-white and grayscale information).

everything from page-layout programs to font and clip-art availability. You also have the option of printing your PostScript-based publication on a professional high-resolution imagesetter when absolute sharpness is required.

The point to keep in mind, though, is that my notes about type handling are specific to PostScript printers. Your mileage may vary, so ask about support for your own printer brand and model before making a purchase decision.

PROGRAMS FOR IBM-COMPATIBLE COMPUTERS

AVAGIO
Version 2.0
$149.95
Unison World, (415) 748-6670
System requirements: 640K PC-compatible (80286 microprocessor or better); hard-disk drive; CGA, EGA, VGA, or Hercules display; mouse; DOS 3.2 or higher; 5/25- or 3.5-inch floppy drive

Rating: ☆ ☆ ☆

In previous releases *Avagio* was strong on flashy graphics and short on desktop publishing basics. In version 2.0, this problem is largely solved, with a substantially improved working environment and the retail price cut in half. There is still a problem using industry-standard font formats, but many laser printer users will be perfectly satisfied with the combination of fonts supplied with the program, and more are available through MicroLogic and Atech. *Avagio* is a particularly strong choice for creating flyers and promotional pieces, where the powerful display type and graphic capabilities can be put to good use.

Pros

Easy and precise object positioning. Clever MiniView makes moving to different areas of layout faster and easier. Complete style sheets. Unusually powerful drawing and text-manipulation tools. Excellent support for color and dot-matrix printers. Master pages, with left and right page differentiation. Text flow around irregular graphics. Autoflow for lengthy text. Headers and footers with automatic numbering. Extensive clip-art library.

Cons

No PostScript or other scalable font support other than *Avagio*'s own format. Must convert bit-mapped fonts (such as HP soft fonts) to *Avagio* format. Won't work with Bitstream fonts at all.

A few compromises but a fine performance overall. I was limited to using Avagio's own fonts, but they print well and included an outline style for the company name. The program's translation utility converted the EPSF waiter to Avagio's own format, but I lost the Caslon typeface and the waiter's tray became narrower and solid black. There were several good-looking frame borders (including our scotch rule) but nothing just right for the coupon, and I lost the hairline rule around Bonnie's picture. Finally, the inability to wrap text around the paw print was a surprise in an otherwise full-featured program.

EXPRESS PUBLISHER
Version 2.0
$159.95
Power Up Software Corporation, (415) 345-5900
System requirements: 640K PC-compatible; mouse recommended; DOS 3.0 or higher; 5.25- or 3.5-inch floppy drive

Rating: ☆ ☆ ☆

Express Publisher makes it simple to jump into desktop publishing. The user interface is clean and easy to grasp, and you can incorporate virtually any word processor or graphic files you own. The scalable Intellifonts print nicely on a variety of printers, and additional fonts are available in this format. However, other fonts are not supported.

Not the least of this program's attractions is the ability to add some graphic pizzazz once you've mastered the basics. *Express Publisher* is well suited for most small business projects, including newsletters, flyers, and brochures, though it's ill equipped for lengthier publications such as books and catalogs.

Pros

Easy-to-use interface, with good manual, tutorial, and on-line help. Timesaving tools to align objects and make them equal in size. Complete style sheets. Produces handsome display type and logos. Very extensive text and graphic file-format import. Good text wrap around irregular graphics. Type-size flexibility for non-PostScript-printer users. Some templates, generous collection of clip art.

Cons

Publications limited to 32 pages. Limited PostScript font support. Not enough magnification levels for viewing document. Doesn't

I couldn't use my PostScript Caslon text font, but at least the waiter graphic with Caslon Openface printed correctly (after much trial-and-error placement with no screen display). I couldn't get proper typographic quotation marks, a significant annoyance. I also couldn't get rid of the crosshatch pattern in the paw print , and frame borders had to be built with drawing tools. On the other hand, the TextEffects module made the "INTRODUCING" banner a snap, and the text wrap looks great.

support facing-page layouts (different left and right page margins, page-number positioning, and so on). No support for TIFF gray-scale scanned images. No master pages.

FINESSE
Version 3.1
$179
Logitech, (415) 795-8500
System requirements: 640K PC-compatible; hard-disk drive; CGA, EGA, VGA, or Hercules display; mouse recommended; DOS 2.1 or higher; 5.25- or 3.5-inch floppy drive

Ratings: ☆ ☆

Finesse looks invitingly simple on screen, with an instinctive design simplicity. Unfortunately in this case, what you see is what you get — a relatively barebones desktop publishing system at about the same price as a more full-featured model. What *Finesse* does it does reasonably well, and you may be perfectly comfortable with it as long as your ambitions remain modest and your publications short. However, when compared to more recently released midrange desktop publishing programs, *Finesse* lacks too many features that make page layout both easier and more graphically exciting to recommend it for frequent use.

Pros

Easy access and quick learning, with on-line help. Includes Bitstream Fontware for fonts in varied sizes. Can scan line art from within program using ScanMan hand scanner. Can copy styles (font and paragraph specifications) from paragraph to paragraph, but has no style sheet. Left and right master pages for repeating elements. Headers and footers with automatic page numbering and date stamping. Some clip art and templates.

Cons

No support of standard font formats other than Fontware. No support for pica measurements. Poor selection of magnifications for

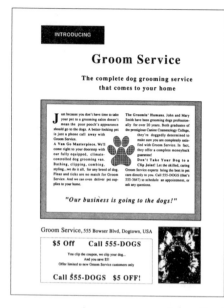

Finesse looks good on screen, but there isn't enough power and flexibility behind that well-designed user interface. I settled for the supplied Dutch font in lieu of Caslon, but even here the typesetting is disappointing (there's far too much letterspacing in the headlines, and fixing that would require adjusting each pair of characters manually). The program won't import EPSF graphics, so the waiter won't serve here. And there was no way to import the paw-print graphic without distorting the fill pattern.

on-screen document viewing. Can't import EPSF graphic files. Loses text formatting during file import. Rotation in 90-degree increments only. Spelling checker sold separately.

MICROSOFT PUBLISHER
Version 1.0
$199
Microsoft Corp., (800) 426-9400
System Requirements: 1-megabyte PC-compatible (80286 micro-processor or better); hard-disk drive; EGA, VGA, or Hercules display; mouse; DOS 3.1 or higher; Microsoft Windows 3.0 or later

Rating: ☆ ☆ ☆ ☆

Microsoft Publisher offers an exceptional combination of friendly yet powerful page-layout features. Text formatting is a strong point, with font sizes available up to 500 points (nearly 7 inches) with .5-point accuracy. The PageWizard automated document creation feature merits special praise. Each PageWizard offers the user a set of publication format and design choices, then creates a document to fit the selections made. There are several worthwhile features missing in this first release, notably the ability to view facing pages on-screen and a stylesheet capability. Overall, though, *Microsoft Publisher* is an excellent program.

Pros

Windows environment provides high degree of compatiblity with user hardware, fonts, graphic file formats, etc. Precise type controls. PageWizard automated document production plus templates. Wide choice of border styles, object shading options. WordArt capability for display type creation. Good, comprehensible manual and on-line help. Master pages.

Cons

No style sheets. Can't view facing pages on-screen. No text wrap around irregular graphics. Substantial hard-disk space requirement.

Putting together the flyer with Microsoft Publisher was very quick work indeed. Thanks to the Windows environment, all of my PostScript fonts were supported, along with the three different graphic file formats required. The rotated "INTRODUCING" was a snap, and the various border styles were just a menu choice away. The only problem: couldn't wrap text around the paw-print graphic.

PFS: FIRST PUBLISHER
Version 3.0
$149
Spinnaker Software, (617) 494-1200
System Requirements: 512K PC-compatible (640K recommended); two drives (hard-disk highly recommended); CGA, EGA, VGA, or Hercules display; mouse; DOS 2.0 or higher; 5.25- or 3.5-inch floppy drive

Rating: ☆

While the rest of the programs in this roundup are solidly midrange, *PFS: First Publisher* teeters precariously on the low end. If you are building single-page layouts with bit-mapped clip art, the program will get the job done. However, the text formatting is borderline for serious business publications. The lack of automatic hyphenation virtually guarantees unattractive word spacing in justified text.

Pros

Can wrap text around irregular graphics. Reasonable text and art import flexibility. Context-sensitive help. Nice system for using simple templates. Text export. Comes with decent selection of clip art. Master pages for repeating page elements.

Cons

No automatic hyphenation. No tabs. No column guides for accurate positioning. Inadequate selection of magnifications for viewing publication. No support for pica measurements. Poor font selection and support. Maximum font size only 48 points. Poor system for resizing graphics. Lacks facing-page document support.

It's clear at a glance that the program wasn't up to the task of creating our sample layout. I used the PostScript printer's built-in Times fonts for lack of other font support and did the best I could with limited tools. The extremely poor scanned image rendition is surprising, since the program does claim to support TIFF files.

Publish It! let me download PostScript fonts (though the italic used in "Our business..." inexplicably prevented the document from printing and had to be deep-sixed). Putting together the page was simple for the most part, but the only way to position the EPSF waiter graphic was through trial-and-error printouts (sorry, no screen display). No rotation for the "INTRODUCING" box or coupon border either, but still a handsome flyer.

PUBLISH IT!
Version 2.0
$249.95
Timeworks, (708) 559-1300
System requirements: 640K PC-compatible; hard-disk drive; CGA, EGA, VGA, or Hercules display; mouse recommended; DOS 3.0 or higher; 5.25- or 3.5-inch floppy drive

Rating: ✩ ✩ ✩

There are many similarities between *Publish It!* and my favorite high-end desktop publishing program, *Ventura Publisher*. However, where *Ventura* is renowned for its high intimidation factor and steep learning curve, *Publish It!* manages to provide several high-end features (notably excellent stylesheets, file import capabilities and font support) in an easy-to-grasp format. While there is still room for improvement, you should be comfortable using *Publish It!* for most business projects, ranging from one-page flyers all the way to lengthy illustrated catalogs.

Pros

Well-designed GEM-based graphical user interface combines simplicity and layout power. Good selection of on-screen magnifications. Well-implemented style sheets. Extensive text and graphic file import, including grayscale TIFF images. Master pages, with left and right margins and headers and footers. Good font support for variety of printers. Scalable typefaces included (but requires creation of soft fonts at each point size, which takes up extra disk space). Text file export. Text wrap around irregular graphics (manual). Good selection of basic drawing tools, fill and line patterns. Generous selection of clip art.

Cons

Lacks spelling checker and thesaurus. Can't scale or crop line art (but can with bit-mapped images). Doesn't display EPSF files on-screen. Can't rotate text or graphics within program.

PROGRAMS FOR MACINTOSH COMPUTERS

PERSONAL PRESS
Version 1.01
$299
Silicon Beach Software /Aldus Corp., (619) 695-6956
System requirements: 1-megabyte Macintosh, two drives (hard-disk drive recommended); System 6.0.5 or higher

Rating: ✩ ✩ ✩ ✩

Personal Press is a textbook example of intelligent software design. You can be loose and freeform when you want (helpful at the initial design stage), then tighten up the publication with little effort and absolute precision. While a bit more expensive than the other programs evaluated, *Personal Press* manages to be midrange without making you feel that you've compromised. Highly recommended for any DTP project, especially those which can make use of the program's powerful template capabilities.

Pros

Excellent user interface, including on-screen previews to display effects of type-styling decisions. Object placement and sizing fast and precise using guidelines, grids, and specification through dialog boxes. Background/master pages; automatic page numbering, time and date stamp. Spelling checker and thesaurus. Extensive grayscale image controls; good color support. Rotate text or graphics to any angle. Unique Autocreate system significantly streamlines template use. Generous selection of file formats for import. Unusually strong file export. Clip-art samples. Superb manual and on-line help.

Cons

All text editing must be done in Actual Size view. Altering style sheet doesn't revise previously styled text. Styles include typeface characteristics only: no alignment or indent, for example.

I created the original version of the sample flyer (see page 51) with Personal Press, the most full-featured of the programs reviewed. I didn't have to make any layout compromises: frame borders, precise object placement on the page, and excellent grayscale image control made building this page a pleasure.

PUBLISH IT! EASY
Version 2.12
$249.95
Timeworks, (708) 559-1300
System requirements: 1-megabyte Macintosh; one drive (hard-disk drive recommended); System 6.0 or higher

Rating: ✩ ✩ ✩ ✩

Another winner in Macintosh midrange desktop publishing. The tools for typesetting control are absolutely first-rate, and the graphics tools let you add spice to your layouts by combining textures, shades, and even color (if you have a color output device) in sophisticated yet easy-to-grasp ways. The addition of a surprisingly slick database manager, well integrated with the rest of the software, is a significant bonus in the latest release of this carefully thought-out, inviting program.

If the program can wrap text around irregular objects, why is the paw-print graphic here sitting in a rectangle? Because the program will only wrap around bitmapped graphics, and using the supplied PICT-to-bitmap conversion seriously corrupted the image quality. The program also came up short in creating the frame borders. Still, I'd be happy distributing this flyer to potential customers.

Pros

Floating tool palettes and command libraries simplify jumping from task to task (especially helpful on small-screen Macintosh models). Fast, precise object placement and sizing using guidelines, grids, and measurement specifications through dialog boxes. Good text wrap-around controls. Excellent drawing tools and fill patterns. Good spelling checker; excellent thesaurus. Rotates text or graphics to any angle. Extensive undo options. Multiple documents open simultaneously (limited only by memory). Complete search and replace functions. Automated page numbering, time and date stamp, page continuation messages. Good manuals and on-line help. Generous selection of text-file formats for import. Text export. Sample art and templates. Sophisticated built-in *File•It!* database module lets user enter, sort, and select data and incorporate it in *Publish It! Easy* documents (including mail-merge printing for personalized individual output).

Cons

Lacks style sheets. Can't turn master pages off for selected individual pages.

PAGE LAYOUT WITH
WORD-PROCESSING SOFTWARE

I received a letter from Patricia Strand in San Jose, California, who uses *WordPerfect* word-processing software and a Hewlett-Packard Deskjet printer to produce newsletters, flyers, price lists, and résumés. Her question: "What am I missing by not using a dedicated desktop publishing system? Am I, in your estimation, a 'real' desktop publisher, or am I guilty of false advertising?"

I have a mental image of Ms. Strand cringing every time there's a knock at the door, afraid the Design Police have finally come to close down her bogus desktop publishing operation. Relax. "Desktop publishing" is essentially a question of output quality. If your clients are happy with the work they're receiving for their desktop publishing dollar, then you're a square shooter in my book.

Are the Design Police going to pinch you? Read on!

However, that doesn't answer her first question: What are you missing out on without special-purpose page-layout software? If your choice to stick with a word processor means you're taking longer to complete each project, or missing out on capabilities that could make your designs look even better, then it could be worth investing the money to buy page-layout software and the time to learn how to use it. Then again, you might find the level of power you need in one of the graphically sophisticated word-processing packages, some of which have incorporated enough page-layout software techniques to satisfy many users.

Let's spend a few minutes exploring the fuzzy boundary line that separates word processing from desktop publishing today.

The Simple Stuff

Basically the complexity of the project should guide your choice of software. Pull a novel off your bookshelf and look at the page-layout requirements: probably just a single column of text, a page number, and a header or footer. There's almost no reason you couldn't produce that book with a simple word-processing program.

Why "almost?" Look at the way text is justified. Different amounts of space have to be added to each line of text so they will all fit the same horizontal measure. Word processors can justify text, but most add the required space between words only. Page-layout software, on the other hand, will add tiny spaces between individual letters as well (called *letterspacing*, to nobody's amazement). Letterspacing helps produce an even, pleasing texture on the page, without leaving excessive gaps in the text lines.

Is that reason enough to leave your word processor behind? That's for your eyes to decide. Of course, if you stick to setting text with a rough right edge, letterspacing won't be a factor at all.

What else is there in a simple, one-column layout that may be difficult to create using a word processor? How about the typeface selection? Some simple word processors are not up to the task of supporting the full range of typefaces your printer may be able to handle, particularly when it comes to additional fonts bought to supplement the built-in selection. As you move into the high-end word-processing arena, though (including Ms. Strand's *WordPerfect* program), this problem essentially vanishes.

Fitting Text Into Columns

I figure we've basically handled two of Ms. Strand's projects fairly successfully with a word processor: price lists and résumés. What new complexities await when producing a newsletter?

There's a good chance your newsletter design will require multiple columns of text. If the text runs in a straight, uninterrupted path, that shouldn't be much of a burden for a word processor capable of producing newspaper-style (sometimes called "snaking") columns. When the text reaches the end of one column, the word processor simply starts again at the top of the following column.

Where it starts getting tricky is a layout where several stories start on a page, with continuations jumping to additional pages. You could create this sort of page using newspaper-style columns, cutting and pasting your text where you desire story breaks, and pasting them together into an artificial order. But that would be an awful lot of trouble.

Let's add another fly to the ointment: illustrations. Newsletters and flyers frequently rely on graphics to convey information or just add graphic interest. Lots of word processors today can incorporate graphics created with various illustration programs, though the number of different formats they support varies widely.

For both discontinuous blocks of text and illustrations, though, we need a way to specify their location on the page. One solution, employed in word processors such as *WordPerfect* on the PC and *Microsoft Word* on the PC and the Macintosh, is to let you specify the position of a selected text block or illustration through a dialogue box, either relative to the page (top centered or bottom right, for example) or by entering specific measurements. This is adequate on a limited basis (for placing a chart in a report, for example), but it becomes cumbersome if you need a more free-form layout.

"I Was Framed!"

That's where the concept of "frames" becomes so useful. A frame is a rectangular box that can hold a block of text or an illustration and be positioned freely on a page. Most desktop publishing programs (including all but one of the examples we've discussed) employ frames in this way.

Frames are no longer the exclusive domain of page-layout programs, though. As graphically oriented software has gained acceptance, several word-processing programs have adopted the frame concept very successfully. They don't require that every piece of text you type be enclosed in a frame — there is a base page that holds everyday straight text. However, when you need to place text blocks or graphic elements independently, you pop a frame on top of that base page and the underlying text moves out of the way to make room for the frame-enclosed material.

To use frames effectively you have to be able to see where you're placing them. That's where a so-called Graphical User Interface (GUI) comes in. The Macintosh, of course, is intrinsically a GUI system, and many MS-DOS users are using Microsoft Windows (and to a lesser extent, GEOS and GEM) to gain a similar kind of what-you-see-is-what-you-get relationship between the image on the screen and the output from the printer. Windows is also very good at handling a variety of fonts (particularly when teamed with Adobe Type Manager or Bitstream Facelift), providing ready access to an enormous selection of available typefaces.

Just because a word processor runs under a GUI does not mean it provides frames for positioning page elements. But those that do make formidable desktop publishing tools.

For example, *Legacy* is a full-featured Windows-based word processor, with all the features that entails (spellchecker and thesaurus, footnotes and endnotes, table of contents and index generation, and so on). However, it is also very well suited for desktop publishing projects, thanks in large part to its implementation of frames. You can fill them with graphics or text and place them wherever you like on a page. You can link text frames so the words will flow to fill them in order and reflow automatically as you edit the text. *Legacy* also boasts word spacing and letterspacing, a graphics toolbox for drawing lines and shapes, and full-featured style sheets to make formatting text faster and more consistent.

Another strong desktop publishing contender among Windows-based word processors is *Ami Pro*, which combines frame-based layout with a useful selection of line and border styles, complete style sheet capability, and a built-in statistical charting package that produces first-rate results.

On the Macintosh side, *WordPerfect 2.0* calls its frames "boxes," but they serve the same purpose: freedom to position sections of text wherever you see fit. The extensive selection of borders offers a quick way to focus reader attention on an item. The drawing tools included are also very useful in a desktop publishing context (especially the free rotation tool that lets you set text or graphics at an angle).

Tough Choices

So, do you stick with your word processor or go out and buy a page-layout program? This is an area where it's easy to be penny wise and pound foolish. There's no shortage of workarounds and tricks to squeeze extra layout mileage from a word-processing package, as the copious selection of volumes on the subject at my local software store will attest. However, as your layouts become more graphically intense and adventurous, it becomes unprofitably time-consuming to create the pages on most word processors. At that point, investing in one of the word processors with strong layout capabilities mentioned above or one of the midrange desktop publishing programs described earlier in this chapter is fully justified by the decreased frustration and increased productivity you'll enjoy.

CHAPTER 4

Start With the Words

"Writing is easy," according to author Gene Fowler. "All you do is sit staring at a blank sheet of paper until the drops of blood form on your forehead." Substitute a blank computer monitor for the sheet of paper and you've described the feelings of many a desktop publisher.

Still, unless you're planning to specialize in coloring books and calendars, the goal of all the graphic and typographic effort you put into your desktop publishing projects is to get somebody to read the text. That's where the meat of the matter lies — your vital information, your irresistible offer, your poignant plea, or your stern warning.

There is no "Writing Made E-Z" method for producing effective text. Each printed piece has a different audience, format, purpose, and style. However, two key qualities consistently distinguish good business communication, whether in a 40-page newsletter or on the back of a matchbook.

Clarity. Your intended readers should find the text easy to understand. Even if the information presented is challenging, the language used should be readily comprehensible.

Accessibility. It should be easy to find the facts, follow them to a logical conclusion, and remember the relevant details.

Here are ten guidelines to help improve the clarity and accessibility of the writing in your DTP projects, whether you are doing the writing yourself or editing someone else's prose.

1. ORGANIZE!

Good writing requires a logical flow of information. Even a simple one-page flyer has to move the reader along in a series of progressive steps. Say you're inviting prospective clients to an informational seminar. You want to:

- **Announce** the seminar;
- **Entice** readers by promising benefits to be gained by attending;
- **Support** your contention that the event is worth their while by summoning up reinforcing facts (a statement of your background and credentials, for example, or a testimonial from a satisfied attendee at a previous event); and
- **Call readers to action** by giving a phone number and offering enticements to produce immediate response (a deadline for reserving a place, for instance, or a cautionary note about limited seating).

What I've done is outline the text I'll need for my flyer. It isn't one of those proper Harvard outlines they taught us in school, with Roman-numeral headings and all that. But even the simple exercise above helps create a logical flow in the final copy.

Outlining is also effective when you are editing text written by someone else. It's often difficult to create a logical flow in a manuscript because the individual points that need to be organized are embedded in large quantities of text. That's why I often prepare a sparse outline as a first step when editing other people's prose. I then cut and paste until my informal outline provides a natural, convincing flow of information. Stripping each paragraph or section down to a few words in outline form makes it easy to juggle ideas and information until they build effectively to a conclusion.

2. SWEAT THE LEAD

If your first paragraph doesn't grab the reader right away, all the good work you do from that point on may be lost. That's reason enough for you to invest all the time it takes to create an effective opener.

What makes a good lead?

Offer an intriguing fact or assertion that immediately engages the reader. "Writing is easy," it says at the top of this chapter. "Oh yeah!" says you, and we're on our way.

Promise a benefit to the reader. "Lose 20 pounds in 20 minutes!" OK, I'm interested.

Deliver an anecdote that encapsulates the reason for reading the ensuing text in personal terms. One of the most famous direct-response ads of all time sold correspondence-school music lessons with the opening line, "They laughed when I sat down at the piano. But when I started to play…!"

A good way to explore the multitude of options for writing an effective lead is to read the material you receive critically. Pay attention to the lead and ask yourself, "Would I keep reading this if I didn't have to?"

3. BREAK UP LONG TEXT BLOCKS

Hold a printout of your text at arm's length and squint at it. If you see lots of different shapes and sizes of paragraphs, you're on the right track. On the other hand, if you're confronted with a series of massive text blocks, it's time to subdivide and conquer by editing into more manageable units.

Lengthy paragraphs may hold information together, but you pay a high price in reader intimidation. Better to find the logical breaking points in your prose and give the reader a break by hitting the carriage return.

Better yet, rephrase lengthy passages with tighter, pithier prose.

The current trend goes beyond merely creating short, punchy paragraphs to packaging entire articles in bite-sized bits — a kind of information McNugget. To achieve this effect in your own publication, consider breaking your material into several stand-alone stories linked under a section or department banner. For a less radical solution, try splitting off a section of a longer story into a stand-alone sidebar, complete with its own headline.

Yet another alternative is to dip into the bag of tried-and-true devices for dividing up text into hors d'oeuvre-size portions: the

Question & Answer format, bulleted lists, checklists, bold subheads, and numbered points (hmm, where have you seen *that* one used lately?).

4. EDIT WITH VISUAL IMPACT IN MIND

As Jan V. White explains in his classic book *Editing by Design* (published by R. R. Bowker Company and highly recommended), text preparation and visual presentation ideally should go hand-in-glove, though this is often not the case. In a nutshell, his prescription for creating more effective communication is to consider what the story will look like on paper *while* it is being written and edited, rather than treating text production and publication design as two entirely separate stages.

There are several practical steps you can take to achieve this end.

Consider ways to deliver information visually. Can you use a chart or graph rather than tediously dishing up facts and figures in body text?

Can you refer to an accompanying illustration and avoid tedious verbal description?

It's also helpful to visualize the page layout as you write. You don't need to design a final layout before the text is written, but you'll save time and effort if you know the project's graphic style while preparing the text.

Do you want a short headline set in large type?

How about a secondary head underneath it?

Do you want to integrate the headline with an illustration?

How will the subheads look, and how many do you want or need?

Will the body text be broken up by graphic elements or be set as straight text?

Your goal is to create a suitable marriage between form and content, and the best place to begin is while creating the content.

5. WRITE TO LENGTH

Writing more text than you have room to print is clearly a waste of valuable time. Not only do you sweat and strain over verbiage destined for deletion, but you have to spend all that extra time cutting what you shouldn't have written in the first place. What's worse, you can lose the clear, logical progression of thought in the oversized original while hacking away at it to fit the available space.

Far better to figure your word count beforehand and write to fit. As a desktop publisher you have an advantage in this regard, since it's a simple matter to slap together a rough layout filled with dummy text and count the words used. Then keep track of your progress while writing by using the word-count feature of your word processor (if it has one). If not, set your margins so each line matches the character count of your layout's column width and count lines as you write.

6. TALK TO YOURSELF

All writing, good and bad, has a narrative voice. The reader hears the words in his or her head and develops a mental image of the business or individual presenting the text.

A handy way to determine whether your text has the voice you want is to close the office door and read it aloud with a critical ear.

Does the tone match the material?

Do you get the sense that a human being wrote this text to be read by other human beings?

Is the voice of your text consistent, or does it veer all over the highway?

Different prose styles are suitable for different occasions. Still, whether my current project is a brief product description or a manual teaching statistical process control, if I can't read a sentence aloud without stumbling and feeling awkward, it isn't a good sentence. Lots of people have a "writing voice" and a "speaking voice" in their prose, and I'm suggesting that often a conversational voice is your best choice.

7. SUMMARIZE

With the exception of certain literary types, good writers don't want to make their readers work hard to understand the point of their work. Summarizing is a useful technique to help a reader along. If there's a product involved, for example, a boxed listing of the points presented in supporting copy can summarize the "hot buttons" that should inspire a purchase.

If the text is lengthy and fairly complex, it often helps to summarize more than once, at natural intervals. Again, a box is often a useful way to set off the summary material.

For more technical projects, a chart or a series of bulleted points can effectively summarize material in a form that will jog the reader's memory and organize the information presented.

8. USE ACTIVE WORDS

Sentence constructions that tend to create tedious reading through their use of excessive verbiage ought to be avoided.

Yuck! Let's try that again.

Avoid wordy sentences.

That's better. By taking the direct approach, I got my information across in a quick, appealing way, without sounding like a self-important twit.

Don't try to make an idea seem more important by throwing more words at it. And watch out for that hobgoblin of sludgy writing, the passive voice, produced by combining the past participle of a verb with the verb "to be." For example:

Passive voice: The zoo was visited by the class.

Active voice: The class visited the zoo.

9. EDIT FOR YOUR AUDIENCE

Understanding your readers' needs and expectations is crucial to successful writing and editing.

How much do they already know about your subject? Defining terms they already understand is nearly as deadly as using unfamiliar vocabulary with no explanation.

At the same time, failing to use the reader's vernacular clearly brands you as an outsider and weakens the effectiveness of your text. The computer consultant trying to drum up business among accountants, for instance, had better learn the phrases accountants use to describe their problems, or the value of the solicitation will depreciate rapidly.

What format are they expecting? If your readers are used to a particular presentation, you'd better have an extraordinarily good reason for feeding them information in another form. Granted, sticking with the tried and true won't always inspire your most sparkling prose or the most attractive publication possible. But there are times when familiarity breeds recognition and respect, and tampering with the formula can backfire.

For example, when a pharmaceutical company asked me to produce some literature describing their new products, I got my hands on their past publications and obediently reproduced both writing style and graphic presentation. Sometimes the best way to communicate is to stimulate and amuse; sometimes it's learning the rules and following them. It all depends on your audience.

10. DON'T LEAVE THEM HANGING

I always find it tempting, after conveying all the information I have on my mind, to simply stop and call it a day. It's more satisfying to the reader, though, if you can come up with a brief, appropriate closing to your text. A good closing might be a call to action, a summary of the information provided, or a restatement and amplification of the original premise of your text.

A good closing indicates that the conversation between writer and reader is over, and the writer didn't leave without saying "goodbye."

But I'm not quite ready to leave the text-building topic yet. Now that we've made your writing as readable as possible, it's time to massage it a bit for easy incorporation in a page-layout program.

PREPARING TEXT FILES FOR DTP

You could write all your text using a desktop publishing program, but it isn't an efficient strategy. The text-editing functions provided in page-layout software are fine for fixing typos and adding the occasional headline or caption, but they're too slow and cumbersome for substantial writing tasks. Writing text with a word processor and importing it into your page-layout software is standard procedure.

So you write the story, save the file, boot up your desktop publishing program, and place the text, right?

Not so fast!

If you linger in your word processor for a few extra minutes, you can save hours of labor. Word processors move through text faster than page-layout programs, offer invaluable search-and-replace functions, and print out quickly for proofreading purposes. Here are several tips for using the strengths of your word processor to stream-line the desktop publishing process.

GET YOUR WRITING RIGHT

Don't wait to proofread your text until it is "set in type" in your page-layout program. You'll save time and aggravation (and do a better job besides) if you read and reread the text carefully at the word-processing stage.

Spelling and Style Checkers

A word processor's spelling checker is your first line of defense against typos. Although an increasing number of DTP programs do include spellcheckers, virtually every leading word processor today offers this useful feature, and often in a more complete and easy-to-use form than the spellchecker found in a page-layout program.

Don't rely exclusively on your computerized spellcheckers, though. Frankly, they're not that smart. If a series of letters spells a word, the spellchecker will accept it as correct, even if those letters don't happen to represent the word you wanted ("the ward you wonted" passed through my spellchecker with flying colors).

While working in your word processor you also have the option of using grammar and style-checking software. I'm not a big fan of these programs. The ones I've used so far still flag lots of perfectly correct text as "potentially" incorrect and rely on the writer to decide whether the prose in question is correct or not. Well if you know enough to second-guess the computer's suggestions, you probably know enough to write it right in the first place! At the same time, I have seen significant improvements among grammar checkers recently, and have to admit that some people swear they make useful proofreading aids. *A chacun son goût* (which sounds much more deliciously pretentious than "to each his own").

Proofreading on Paper

When proofreading a word-processing file, I do a better job working with a printout, rather than reading directly from the screen. I also strongly suggest proofreading text printed out in plain old typewriter-style Courier type with double-spaced lines, no matter what typeface you'll be using in the final publication. Courier is a monospaced font — that means each letter has the same width, as opposed to proportional fonts such as Times and Helvetica in which characters are spaced according to the width of the actual letters. You are more likely to miss spelling errors involving skinny letters such as "i" and "l" when they are printed in a proportional font.

Of course, you'll still have to proofread your publication once it's laid out with your desktop publishing software, looking for poor hyphenation, bad column breaks and so on. But at least you'll know the text arrived in good condition.

TYPOGRAPHIC NICETIES

There are several typographic differences between typewritten and typeset text. You can make these changes in your desktop publishing program, but it's much more efficient to handle them with your word processor.

Single-Spaced Sentences

We all learned to hit the spacebar twice at the end of a sentence. That's fine for typewritten text, but wrong for typesetting, where the extra space can leave unsightly gaps (especially in justified text). You can try reminding yourself to single-space as you type, but it's much simpler to use your word processor's search-and-replace function to search for all the double spaces and replace them with single spaces.

Spaces Between Paragraphs

Adding extra space between paragraphs by hitting the Return (or Enter) key twice is a common typing practice. If you want space between paragraphs in your final publication, insert it using the page-layout program's spacing controls instead. You'll get finer spacing control, and won't find unwanted blank lines at the tops or bottoms of columns when paragraph endings coincide with column breaks.

Check your word-processing software manual for the procedure used to search-and-replace carriage return characters (this varies from program to program), then replace double returns with single returns.

Typographic Quotes, Apostrophes, and Dashes

The quotation mark and apostrophe characters on your keyboard are holdovers from typewriter days — typewriters don't offer properly shaped single and double open and closed quotation marks, much less a respectable apostrophe. But when it comes to creating professional-looking desktop-published documents, you'll need the typographically correct punctuation included in most printer fonts.

Similarly, we often type two hyphens to represent a dash in typewritten text. In your typeset copy use a real dash (called an *em dash* because it's about the same width as the capital letter "M").

Should you include a space before and after a dash? I prefer including the space, but you'll see it both ways — it's a matter of style. For this book I have used a space to separate my em dashes from the surrounding text, despite the fact that my publisher's standard style omits the spaces. Whatever you decide, the important point is to be consistent, and your word processor's search capabilities will help ensure this consistency.

On typewriters we also use hyphens to indicate a numerical range — for instance, 2-4 inches. The typographically correct character is an *en dash* (2–4 inches).

Macintosh users will find it easy to substitute typographically correct characters for their typewriter equivalents because the characters are readily available from the keyboard using standardized Option and Shift key combinations. Check your word-processing or page-layout software manual, or use the Key Caps desk accessory to find the proper key combinations. You can type the characters correctly as you write, or use search and replace later. Note that, to transform quotation marks correctly, you'll have to include the space before or after the mark in your search.

These substitutions are trickier for MS-DOS users because the keystrokes required are not standardized between different programs. However, many word processors and page-layout programs for PC-compatibles do support the typographically correct characters, with the appropriate keystrokes listed in the reference manual.

A few desktop publishing programs will handle some or all of these typographical conversions for you automatically. For example, *Publish It!* on the PC and *Publish It! Easy* on the Macintosh will automatically convert double hyphens to em dashes, insert correct opening and closing quotation marks, and strip out extra carriage returns between paragraphs. However, this is the exception rather than the rule.

STYLISH IMPORTS

One of the most time-consuming chores in preparing page layouts is selecting text blocks and indicating the font and spacing you want. It requires scrolling through the entire publication, using your mouse to select the text, then pulling down one or more menus to make your typographical choices. Even if your desktop publishing software supports keyboard shortcuts for these tasks, it's still slow going and easy to make mistakes. You can make the process much easier using your word-processing software.

The ideal solution is to look for highly compatible word processing/desktop publishing software combinations. Any page-layout program will accept plain, unformatted ASCII text files, but most will also import files from selected word processors with some or all of their formatting, such as boldfaced and italicized type, intact.

The Style Sheet Shortcut

Several high-performance word processors and desktop publishing applications use style sheets — named combinations of formatting choices including typeface and size. One reason that *Microsoft Word* and *Personal Press* make an especially appealing desktop publishing combination on the Macintosh is the fact that their style sheets are compatible. A *Word* file complete with style sheet can be imported into *Personal Press* fully formatted, and the styles you created in *Word* can then be edited in *Personal Press* if changes are necessary.

Knowing the Codes

Even without style sheet compatibility, you can sometimes insert codes in your word-processing file to apply styles automatically when a document is imported.

For example, if you define a style called "Subhead" in a *Publish It!* document, you can enter <Subhead> (including the brackets) in any word-processed text file, and the words following the code will automatically assume the Subhead specifications when you import the file.

Sometimes you can save time with precoding even with a page-layout program that doesn't offer style sheet capability. *PFS: First Publisher*, for example, does not support stylesheets, but it does allow you to insert font specifications in your text files with the *FONT* command. For example, if you insert the phrase *FONT Geneva 14 bold* in your text file, the text that follows will be set in Geneva 14-point bold until the next *FONT* command appears.

At first glance it may appear that typing in coding instructions in your word-processing file is about as much trouble as styling the text on-screen in your desktop publishing program. But if your word processor is one of the many that supports macros, you can define simple keystroke combinations that will insert the entire coding phrase quickly and with perfect consistency. Even without macros, you can use search and replace to achieve the same end. In the *First Publisher* example, you might type "GN" before each Geneva 14-point bold text block, then quickly change them all to the full coding string using your word processor's search-and-replace function.

LEARNING THE SHORTCUTS

Traditional computer-based typography relies exclusively on codes embedded in a text file to style a page. Although these programs offer excellent typographic control, graphically based desktop publishing software that displays a page accurately on-screen is much simpler to use and provides better design feedback while you work. However, by taking a little time to adopt a few simple coding practices, the page that appears on your computer screen when you import your text will be much closer to the final version than it would if you simply imported plain text files. Since each desktop publishing software program has its own conventions, this requires a little hunting in the reference manual. However, that one-time investment in learning the shortcuts pays off in consistent and considerable time savings on every desktop publishing project you undertake.

CHAPTER 5

Getting the Type Right

When you set up a desktop publishing system, you enter a community of typesetters and designers that goes back to the days when printed pages were composed by arranging individually cast pieces of metal type in a large wooden frame.

We inherit more than tradition from our ink-stained forebears. We also inherit a vocabulary that is still used today in all kinds of typesetting, whether mechanical or computerized. Desktop publishing software makes choosing and using type relatively simple. However, there are still a number of key concepts and terms rooted in traditional typography that you'll need to understand when tackling desktop publishing tasks.

FOR GOOD MEASURE

Let's start by using the proper word for the job at hand. A designer doesn't "choose" type — he or she *specs* type. Pronounced "specks," it's short for "specifies," and the resulting instructions to the typesetter are the "type specs" or "type specifications."

Good old inches are widely used in setting up page sizes and margins, but typesetting also employs two publishing-specific units of measure: *picas* and *points*.

The point system of type measurement was invented in 1737 by a French typographer named Pierre Simon Fournier, and it became an international standard. Each point is precisely .013837 inch, which for all practical purposes means there are 72 points to the inch. Measurements of type height and the space between lines of type are expressed in points. The main text of *No-Sweat Desktop Publishing* is set in 11-point Adobe Caslon with three additional points between the lines.

That space between lines of type is called *leading* (pronounced "ledding"). The term is a holdover from the days when individual strips of lead were inserted between lines of metal type. When we say type is "set solid," we mean there is no additional leading inserted between lines. This does not mean the bottom of one line of letters touches the top of the one beneath it, since there is some spacing on the top and bottom built into the typeface definition.

When we add space between lines, we add a point or two of leading. If we set 10-point type without any additional leading, we say it's set "10 on 10," which is often written 10/10. With one point of leading it's 10 on 11, or 10/11. The text you're reading here is 11 on 14, or 11/14.

Larger measurements, such as the width of a column or page and column margins, are expressed in picas. One pica equals 12 points. Since there are 72 points to the inch and 72 divided by 12 equals 6, there are 6 picas to the inch (within a hair's breadth).

It is not uncommon to see mix-and-match measurement units in page-layout specifications since paper is usually ordered in inches, and typography is usually set up in pica widths. Most designers find it simplest to translate the page dimensions to picas just once, and spec the column widths and margins in picas.

Tekton, 8 point
Tekton, 10 point
Tekton, 14 point
Tekton, 24 point
Tekton, 30 point

Above are samples of the Tekton typeface set in five point sizes.

This is a sample of the Times typeface set in 12-point size without additional leading, or "12 on 12."

This is a sample of the Times typeface set in 12-point size with 2 points of additional leading, or "12 on 14."

The type size in both samples at left is the same, but the difference in leading has a substantial effect.

Another piece of jargon you may encounter is a *measure*, which is synonymous with "column width" in typesetting terms. If you set a column of text 16 picas wide, you've set it to a measure of 16 picas. The measure of the column you are now reading is 25.5 picas.

EMS AND ENS

No, they're not color-coated candies — *ems* and *ens* are useful typographic measurements. An em is the width of the capital "M" in a particular typeface, and an en is the width of the "N."

Since these measurements vary for different type sizes, they are useful for specifying dimensions that need to be in proportion to the type characters. For example, an em dash is a dash the width of an "M" — same idea with an en dash, an em space, and an en space. An em dash is used in 'the preceding sentence to emphasize the break in the text flow.

TYPEFACE VS. FONT

A *typeface* is the design of a particular set of letters, symbols, and punctuation marks. Helvetica, Times, Palatino, and Optima are typefaces. Sometimes when we talk about typefaces we really mean typeface *families*. Times Roman, Times Bold, Times Italic, and Times Bold Italic are all different typefaces in the Times family that share the same underlying characteristics, but require a separate design for each weight or slant.

Traditionally, a font is a complete set of type for a single typeface in a single size. Therefore, 12-point Helvetica and 10-point Helvetica are different fonts. This distinction is still significant to users of non-PostScript printers, which require a separate font definition for each type size. PostScript printers, on the other hand, allow the user freedom to scale the size of the typeface up and down, blurring the distinction between typefaces and fonts.

This muddled jargon helps explain the confusion encountered by some laser-printer shoppers when they try to compare the number of built-in typefaces (often referred to as "fonts" in advertising) in different printers. Most PostScript printers now include a standardized assortment of thirty-five typefaces. When you look at the list, though, you generally find only ten typeface names. That's because

Times Roman
Times Bold
Times Italic
Times Bold Italic

When you shop for a printer, each version of Times shown above is counted separately when calculating the number of typefaces included.

most of these ten actually include several members of a typeface family. Palatino, for example, is provided in roman (straight up and down in medium weight), italic (slanted), bold, and bold italic. That's four typefaces.

TWO TYPES OF TYPE

A graphic artist may have 1,000 typefaces or more from which to choose. Although only a fraction of these have been adapted for laser printers, the variety is impressive and at times daunting. How do you distinguish among typefaces?

First, split them into two groups. On one side is *serif* type. Serifs are those little decorative lines and curves at the ends of letters. The most commonly used serif type in desktop publishing is Times (called "Dutch" by some typeface publishers).

Then there are the faces without serifs, called *sans serif* type (*sans* is French for "without"). The most familiar sans serif type in desktop publishing is Helvetica (sometimes called Swiss).

Tradition holds that serifs help hold a block of text together visually, making it easier for the eye to follow along the line of type. Thus, serif type is used frequently for lengthy blocks of text (often called *body copy*), while sans serif is used for heads, subheads, captions, and short text blocks. That's tradition, of course, not law. If you want a very modern look, you may well choose sans serif type for body copy.

BOLD, ITALIC, AND CONDENSED TYPEFACES

Next we'll look at the weight of the characters — that is, the thickness of the lines that make up the letters. Here again, commercial typography provides more variety than laser type. Letters with thicker lines are called *boldface*. There may be six or more gradations of boldness available in a commercial typeface family such as Garamond, from light to ultra bold. So far, we are limited to a single bold version for most laser-based typefaces. Some bold laser fonts are darker than others, though, and this may be a reason to choose one font over another for a given project. And selected laser-based typefaces have been designed in families with four or more steps of boldness to provide maximum design flexibility. Boldface type is best used for subheads (as in the headings for this book) or for other forms of emphasis.

The forward slant in type, called *italic*, is another distinction. Frequently there is more variation between the italic versions of two different typefaces than between the standard, or *roman*, versions of the same typefaces, particularly with serif type. If you are planning to use a lot of italic type in a particular job, you might choose your typeface based on the look of its italic.

Many typefaces also come in a condensed version, in which the width of the letters has been compressed. No condensed fonts are included in the basic typeface packages delivered with today's laser printers, but they're available as downloadable fonts. Condensed faces are frequently useful if you need to fit more letters into a narrow width, particularly for headlines and subheads.

THE VISUAL TERMINOLOGY OF TYPEFACES

A closer look at the shapes of the letters will reveal subtle but significant differences among typefaces. In order to pick the best typeface for the job at hand, here are a few points to look for when you spec type.

Variation Between Thin and Thick Strokes

The weight of strokes differs considerably from typeface to typeface and contributes a great deal to their personalities. Generally, a typeface constructed with strokes that don't vary much in width appears less elegant and more straightforward, calling less attention to itself than a typeface with letter shapes that vary in thickness. On the other hand, 300-dpi laser printing can't accurately reproduce the fine strokes of some typefaces.

Height of Lowercase Letters

The lowercase letters of different faces differ in height in proportion to the capitals. Lowercase letter size is referred to as x-height, since "x" is a convenient letter to measure, without *ascenders* (such as the vertical line in a "b" or "d") or *descenders* (the part of a "p" or "g" that's below the rest of the letters). A typeface with a large x-height will appear larger on the page than a smaller x-height face, even when both are set in the same point size.

Different Serif Shapes

Some typefaces, such as Times, have finely curved serifs (*bracket* serifs). Others, like Memphis, have squared-off serifs (*slab* serifs). Palatino, part of the standard typeface package built into most laser printers, has triangular-shaped serifs (*wedge* serifs), while a typeface like Walbaum has serifs consisting of simple fine lines (*hairline* serifs). Note that some serif shapes are more clean-cut (bracket or triangular), and others are more ornamental (hairline).

Design Distinctions

When you look closely at type samples, you quickly begin to spot design distinctions. How round are the *counters* (those open areas in the "B," "R," "P," etc.)? Does the lowercase letter "g" have a circular descender or a simpler stroke? How ornamental is the capital "Q"?

These "closer looks" are more than an interesting exercise; they're the key to typographic detective work. One way to create attractive typography is to find examples of professional design you admire and identify the typefaces used for future reference in your own desktop publishing projects. By minding your p's and q's (and other telltale letters, such as lowercase "a," "f," "g," and "y"), you should be able to compare printed material to samples of type in a catalog and make the identification.

LOOKING YOUR BEST AT 300 DOTS PER INCH

The standard resolution for laser printer output today is 300-dpi — that is, a maximum of 300 individual dots of toner can be placed side by side for each inch horizontally, with 300 of these rows stacked in each vertical inch. Compared to your computer monitor, which displays about 72 dots per inch, the laser printer is an extraordinarily high-resolution device. Compared to a professional typesetting system, it stinks.

Sorry, but anybody with a pocket calculator can quickly see that laser printers are simply in a different class from true typesetting

Times has bracket serifs.

Memphis features slab serifs.

Palatino serifs are wedge-shaped.

Walbaum has hair-line serifs.

machines, which provide a standard output resolution of over 1,200 dots per inch, and can produce over 2,500 dots per inch if needed. (The type for his book was output at 1,270 dots per inch.)

Laser printer: 90,000 dots in a square inch. Phototypesetter: 1,440,000 dots in a square inch, or over 6,000,000 at higher resolution settings.

No, I'm not a nattering nabob of negativity. I love my laser printer and turn out good work with it. But the first step to making the most of your laser-printed output is to understand its limitations. Then we can work at compensating for them.

Where do we start? By choosing typefaces that reproduce well at laser printer resolution.

BEYOND THE TYPE CATALOG

There are two kinds of laser-printer type: fixed-size fonts and scalable type.

Fixed-size fonts are commonly used for laser printers like the Hewlett-Packard LaserJet Series II, which requires a different font file for each size of type. If you buy 10-point Times you can print 10-point Times, but not 12-point Times — that requires a different font file.

One advantage of fixed-size fonts, though, is that when you thumb through a catalog, you see reasonably accurate reproductions of what will come out of your own laser printer. The same can't be said for scalable type.

There are many varieties of scalable type, including Adobe's PostScript format, Bitstream's Speedo format, and Atech's Publisher's Powerpak typefaces. If you are using a scalable font, you don't need separate font files for different point sizes. Instead you get a single font description file that the software uses to produce type at virtually any size you request.

A significant advantage of scalable typefaces: they can be used on anything from dot-matrix printers to high-resolution imagesetters (with varying degrees of output quality, of course). However, this becomes a disadvantage when shopping for type.

The samples in any scalable type catalog I've ever seen are printed using high-resolution output. But the difference between that sample and laser-printed output can be dramatic.

Times:
R P Q p q a f g y

Adobe Caslon:
R P Q p q a f g y

Walbaum:
R P Q p q a f g y

Palatino:
R P Q p q a f g y

Rotis Serif:
R P Q p q a f g y

Trying to identify a typeface sample? Look for instances of "telltale" letters like those shown above.

What are the type characteristics you should scrutinize most carefully when evaluating typefaces for laser printer output?

Fine Lines

A 300-dpi laser printer can't reproduce the thinnest lines of many typeface designs. This includes very light faces, and the thin hairline strokes found in the serifs of many fonts. Some type designs depend on extreme differences between the thick and thin parts of the letterform for their effect. Bodoni is a good example. Others are more subtly shaped, like the swelling and thinning lines that make up the letters in the Optima face. These faces look great in a type catalog but lose their punch in laser-printed output.

Curves

The curved characters in a laser-printed font often look like they need a shave. This "stubble" is more apparent in some fonts and sizes than others, a variation you can't predict by looking at high-resolution output in a type catalog.

Diagonals

Laser printers do their best work with straight vertical and horizontal strokes. Ask them to print a line at an angle and the results are unpredictable. This problem is especially noticeable in italic fonts, which are, by definition, slanted.

Enclosed Spaces

Type designs vary widely in the shape of the counters (the enclosed space in the letter shape) in letters like "e," "a," and "q." When laser-printing a font with small counters in small point sizes, the area is likely to fill up completely, particularly with lowercase "e" and "a."

Laser-Printed Samples

Some of these problems can be predicted fairly reliably just by looking at the type catalog (thin lines or small counters, for instance). However, the only way to know with absolute certainty whether a font will reproduce attractively on your laser printer is to get a laser-printed sample, at the size and weight you need. It's a bit of a bother, but most service bureaus (including many of the nationally franchised quick-print and copy shops) offer laser-printed output and have a good selection of fonts on hand. Considering the fact that fonts typically cost over $100 (and some over $300), the extra effort to get a proper sample before buying seems well justified.

SOME FONT RECOMMENDATIONS

Based on my own meanderings through the world of laser-printed type, I have some specific typefaces to recommend.

First, you have a fairly free hand when it comes to choosing type to be used in large sizes for headlines. Once you get to about 18 points in height, laser-printed type in most faces starts to look pretty good (though you'll still lose the fine details found in high-resolution output of the same fonts). The relative simplicity of most sans serif typefaces, which lack the fine strokes usually used to create serifs, make them especially good choices for laser reproduction at large point sizes.

If you're looking for text face variety beyond the typefaces built into your laser printer, check out the fonts developed by Adobe and Bitstream especially for laser printer output. By skillfully using curves and line weights that reproduce well at 300 dpi, their designers have created several attractive, workhorse fonts.

Bitstream's Charter is a good example of a text face that works well in small sizes. The serifs are reasonably thick, the counters are open, and even the italics keep the stairstep effect commonly found in diagonal strokes to a minimum.

Adobe's Stone series offers a complete family of fonts custom-designed for laser printing that work harmoniously together. There is ITC Stone Serif, Stone Informal (another serif face), and Stone Sans Serif. Taken together, they offer all the weight and style variations you might need for newsletters, books, or brochures.

Two more attractive Adobe serif fonts designed with laser printers in mind are Lucida and Utopia. I've been using a lot of Utopia lately — it's a solid, straightforward face that I find very inviting and readable in long text settings.

Charter 12 pt. ABCDEFGHIJKabcdefghijkabcdefghijk1234567890
Charter 18 pt. ABCDEFGHIJKabcdefghijklmnopqrstuv
Stone 12 pt. ABCDEFGHIJKabcdefghij*abcdefghijk*1234567890
Stone 18 pt. ABCDEFGHIJKabcdefghij*abcdefghijkl*
Lucida 12 pt. ABCDEFGHIJabcdefghij*abcdefghij*1234567890
Lucida 18 pt. ABCDEFGHIJabcdefghij*abcdefghij*
Utopia 12 pt. ABCDEFGHIJKabcdefghij*abcdefghijk*1234567890
Utopia 18 pt. ABCDEFGHIJKabcdefghij*abcdefghijk*

These four typefaces were specially designed to reproduce well at 300 dpi. The samples shown here were output on a Hewlett-Packard LaserJet with a PostScript cartridge.

Among serif faces not specifically designed with laser printing in mind, the ones that seem to work best have fairly even widths and large counters, such as Century Old Style and Century Schoolbook, Centennial, Melior and good old Times Roman. If you want a face with more distinctive character, look for type with graphic flourishes pronounced enough to hold up at relatively low resolution. Clearface and Korinna are good examples of highly styled faces that work well when laser-printed.

A FEW MORE TIPS

Once you've selected a typeface that prints out well, there are a few more steps you can take to maximize reproduction quality.

Adjust the Toner Density

Try moving the toner density setting of your laser printer a notch or two toward the lighter side. The default setting for toner density often favors producing solid black areas over maintaining type detail. Often a lighter setting will produce better results for type reproduction (and make your toner cartridge last longer besides). But keep in mind that you may not see the result of a toner density setting adjustment until you've run a few sheets through the printer.

Reduce Your Printouts

A quick trick to improve final quality is to print the original larger than the final piece and reduce it for reproduction, effectively increasing the number of dots per inch. Of course, you'll have to increase the type size and leading proportionally. For example, instead of printing out 11-point type with 12-point leading, use 22-point type on 24-point leading and reduce the resulting printout by 50 percent. That may require printing the page in sections and aligning them on an oversize mounting board.

Use Bright White Paper

When it comes to paper, there are all kinds of "white." You want to print your ready-for-reproduction originals on opaque, bright-white stock to maximize contrast. I generally use Hammermill's Laser Plus paper for this purpose. You'll pay premium prices for these specialty papers (about $20 for 250 sheets), but a little goes a long way, and the results are worth it.

Speak With Your Print Shop Professional

If you will be sending your publication to a professional print shop for reproduction, ask them to adjust their camera for optimal results. A good printer will know how to capture as much detail as possible while minimizing the type imperfections that appear.

Also discuss the paper stock your job will print on; some are more forgiving of low-resolution originals than others.

TAP THE GRAPHIC POWER OF DISPLAY TYPE

Sometimes you want a type treatment that really calls attention to itself, particularly in large headlines. You might want to set the headline for a fur salon advertisement in a typeface that reeks of elegance and sophistication. Or you may be printing flyers promoting a Halloween costume sale and want a headline that reeks of cobwebs and slime. In either case, you're entering the world of display type.

Display type, generally used to set headlines and titles and to create logos, differs in several ways from body type. At the most elementary level, it's set larger than straight text. On a more utilitarian level, it serves a more dramatic function, communicating a strong message through the visual impact of unusual and distinctive lettering. And with desktop publishing technology, display type is a perfect area for experimenting, stretching your creative muscles, and just having some fun.

Why Use Display Type?

You don't have to use display type at all. In fact, in a project such as an annual report or a financial newsletter, you may want the conservative feel provided by using body type in a larger size for the headlines and subheads.

More often, however, you want titles and major heads to do more than just deliver the text. You want to attract attention. You want to deliver a message about the contents of a book, brochure, advertisement, or article by choosing typefaces that elicit an emotional response. Peruse the shelves of your local bookstore and consider the extraordinary variety and cleverness of the typography on book jackets and the multitude of ways in which you are encouraged to judge a book by its cover. This is the art of display typography.

Making the most of display type's power to attract and amuse begins with a wide selection of typefaces. Do you want to run the headline for your Back-to-School catalog in a typeface that resembles the team letters worn by college athletes? Do you think the headlines in a travel brochure about Japan should have an oriental flavor? Whether your taste runs toward cliché or true cleverness, sift through a generous catalog of fonts to find the typeface that evokes just the right mood and message.

Since display type is often suitable for a special purpose in a particular project, you may not want to spend between $100 and $300 on a typeface you'll rarely, if ever, use again. There are lower-cost alternative sources of display type to consider.

Some computer illustration programs come complete with a generous selection of display typefaces. *CorelDRAW* for IBM-compatible computers, for instance, includes over 150 typefaces well suited for creating display type treatments.

There are also collections of typefaces created specifically for

These display type samples were created very quickly using the TypeStyler program on a Macintosh computer.

display type applications available at reasonable prices. *FontBank*, for example, offers a complete library of 250 PostScript typefaces in both IBM-compatible and Macintosh formats for under $200.

An additional source of low-cost display typefaces are the on-line bulletin boards available to modem-equipped computer users. You will find a wealth of unusual and often surprising typefaces offered as *shareware*. That means you can download the typeface to your computer and try it out in your layout. If you choose to use it, you are expected to submit a modest fee to the creator, on the honor system.

Finally, there are special-purpose desktop publishing programs for creating display type. These programs, such as *TypeStyler* and *LetraStudio*, come with substantial libraries of attractive typefaces suitable for display work. But they go beyond simply setting the letters in large sizes on a straight line. They offer the ability to reshape and manipulate letters to create unique graphic effects.

Display Type Then and Now

Many applications of display type use letterforms as artistic design elements that can be radically modified to achieve an effect. Look at company logos and, once again, at book jackets. Has the designer elongated a portion of a letter, or rotated type at an intriguing angle, or closely connected letters to form appealing shapes?

There are two ways to achieve these effects using traditional methods. One is to order custom type from a phototypesetter or use rub-down transfer type (Letraset's Instant Library is the most common source) to create the basic lettering, and then manipulate that initial setting using special cameras with distorting lenses.

The other alternative is to hire an accomplished artist to create the display lettering by hand. In either case, achieving mechanically precise lines in display type often requires laborious retouching or preparing the original artwork at drastically enlarged sizes and radically shrinking it for reproduction.

Making sophisticated display type creation available through personal computer software, however, is a major breakthrough for both the professional designer and the enthusiastic amateur. The computer relieves the professional of the tedious work involved in preparing display type. The process becomes interactive, enabling you to use the on-screen display and laser-printed proofs to achieve the desired effect far more quickly and economically than before.

And using display type creation software, the amateur moves into a realm that was formerly closed off altogether by the twin requirements of special equipment and manual dexterity.

CHAPTER 6

Getting the Picture

For the most part, desktop publishing eliminates the need for manual dexterity in assembling pages for publication. You can even use page-layout software to draw basic lines or shapes that are more precise than those a skilled graphic artist could draw by hand, and take far less time to complete the job.

That's fine for creating rules, boxes, and circles, but it's not much help when you want a picture of Santa for your December issue, or a flower to illustrate a gardening story, or small images of credit cards to drop into an order form.

Of course, the traditional approach still works fine when you need illustrations for a publication. If you are a capable artist, render the illustration you want using pen and ink, or paint. You can then either incorporate the result into your publication using an image scanner or hand the original over to the print shop to incorporate in the final printing films. The same is true for photographic illustrations: Take the picture yourself or hire a pro to do it, then reproduce it using a scanner or a professional print shop.

Some artistically inclined individuals will find success using computer-based illustration programs. These powerful software tools still won't endow their users with artistic talent, but they do offer two enormous benefits that trickle down to even profoundly mediocre draftsmen.

First is the ability to erase cleanly and perfectly, and redo anything from major sections to minor details as often as necessary.

Second is the freedom to view your artwork at a variety of magnifications. You might not have the manual dexterity to put the gleam in the eye of a face you're drawing when it's only an inch across on a piece of paper, but computer illustration software allows you to zoom in on that eye until it fills the screen. That removes much of the manual dexterity requirement from creating artwork. But of course, you still need underlying artistic ability to create a high-quality illustration, on paper or on computer.

As a desktop publisher, though, you have a few additional resources at your disposal that allow you to add handsome graphics to your publications without hiring outside illustrators or reproducing your own modest efforts for the world to see. In this chapter we'll explore three of these options:

- Professionally prepared clip art;
- Computer-generated tables and charts; and
- Scanned illustrations and photographs.

CLIP ART: A READY-TO-USE RESOURCE

The clip-art concept didn't start with desktop publishing. Publishers have long relied on books and subscription services to provide ready-to-run artwork, either old enough to be free of copyright protection or newly created and licensed to the purchasers for inclusion in their publications. It's called *clip* art because you can just clip it out and paste it down on your camera-ready mechanical.

There's no reason desktop publishers can't use printed clip art in exactly the same way as their more tradition-bound cohorts. However, we have another rich art resource at our disposal in the form of disk-based collections of graphic images. Computerized clip art is at once more flexible and more complex than paper artwork — flexible because the artwork can be easily sized and altered right on the computer, complex because of the variety of file formats and image resolutions available for both IBM-compatible and Macintosh computers.

PostScript clip art can be resized to your heart's content without affecting the line quality of the image

FITTING THE FORMAT TO YOUR NEEDS

Clip art is widely available in three formats:

• Bitmapped graphics such as *MacPaint* files for the Macintosh or *PC Paintbrush* files (PCX format) for IBM-compatible systems;

• Object-oriented drawings, such as the PICT file format used in *MacDraw* for the Macintosh or CGM files used by *Harvard Graphics* for IBM-compatibles;

• PostScript artwork, created with programs such as *Adobe Illustrator* or *Aldus Freehand* on the Macintosh and *CorelDRAW* or *Micrografx Draw* on IBM-compatibles. PostScript artwork can only be output on PostScript-equipped printers or imagesetting equipment.

Most page-layout software will accept illustrations in all three kinds of formats. However, there are advantages and disadvantages to each.

Bit-Mapped Graphics

Bit-mapped graphics are dot-by-dot representations of pictures. These images are created to print at a specific resolution; generally either 72 dpi (the resolution of the Macintosh screen and Apple Computer's ImageWriter printer) or 300 dpi (the resolution of most laser printers).

Bit-mapped images are easy to edit. Just load them into a compatible paint program and manipulate them dot by dot. They are also less expensive than other clip-art formats. In fact, such images are widely available in the public domain (meaning no charge to the user) from computer user groups and on-line bulletin boards.

The tricky part comes when you try to change the size of a bit-mapped graphic. Enlarging an image spreads out the dot pattern, adversely affecting the graphic quality. Shrinking it may produce jagged edges and blotchy sections, particularly if there are patterned areas involved.

Object-Oriented and PostScript Drawings

Both object-oriented graphic images and PostScript graphics consist of a computerized description of the lines required to make up the images, rather than a dot-by-dot bitmap. That means you can change the size of the image freely and even distort it horizontally or vertically without degrading the quality of the lines. Also, these images will print out at the maximum resolution offered by your output device. Those curves and slanted lines that print out decently on your laser printer will be entirely smooth and sharp if you print the file on high-resolution imagesetting equipment.

An image in pure PostScript format will not display on-screen in your desktop publishing application. To solve this problem, a standardized format called Encapsulated PostScript Files (EPSF) was established. EPSF files, available in both Macintosh and PC-compatible versions, include both the PostScript description of the image (which goes to the computer printer) and a bit-mapped screen image that lets you place, size, and crop the picture within your page-layout program.

Another advantage of the EPSF format standard is that both Macintosh and PC-compatible programs will accept the same file. However, the bit-mapped images used for display on your screen are not interchangeable between the two systems. If you load a Macintosh EPSF file into your PC-based page-layout program, you'll see a blank box on screen where the picture should be. However, the printable PostScript code will be sent to the computer printer with the rest of the page and reproduce accurately.

BROWSING THE CLIP-ART COLLECTIONS

You will rarely find an extensive selection of clip art on your local software store's shelves. The best way to shop around is to call or write for catalogs directly from the publishers, then order by mail. Here are samples from a few high-quality disk-based clip-art vendors.

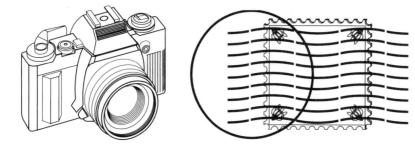

Sample EPSF images from the T/Maker catalog.

T/MAKER, 1390 Villa Street, Mountain View, CA 94041; (415) 962-0195. T/Maker offers *Clickart* collections for both Macintosh and PC-compatible computers, in both EPSF and bit-mapped formats. These range from business images to holiday illustrations and even religious graphics.

METRO IMAGEBASE, 18623 Ventura Boulevard, Suite 210, Tarzana, CA 91356; (800) 525-1552. Metro ImageBase is best known for its stylish, highly detailed bit-mapped graphics. Unlike some bit-mapped art, the ImageBase offerings are 300-dpi graphics. They can be placed in all of the popular page-layout programs, though editing these files requires a 300-dpi-compatible graphics program. The company now also offers several volumes of handsome EPSF images. All Metro ImageBase graphics are available in both Macintosh and PC-compatible file formats.

Metro Imagebase offers a wide selection of bit-mapped images (including the hourglass above) and some EPSF-format graphics, including the CELEBRATION banner from the company's Headings package.

DUBL-CLICK SOFTWARE, 9316 Deering Avenue, Chatsworth, CA 91311; (818) 700-9525. The *WetPaint* bit-mapped graphics collections from Dubl-Click include several volumes of crisp, modern designs and others consisting of digitized versions of old-fashioned engravings. The Macintosh-only disks include an excellent desk-accessory graphics program called *Art Roundup* at no additional cost.

The Printer's Helper volume in Dubl-Click's WetPaint series includes attractive ready-to-fill frames like this one, taken from old engravings.

Image Club's Fabulous Fifties collection creates a mood instantly — but if you prefer more modern-looking cartoons, the company offers several volumes.

IMAGE CLUB GRAPHICS, 1902 11th Street SE, Calgary, Alberta, T2G 3G2, Canada; (403) 262-8008. While not all of the *Digit-Art* EPSF and PICT file collections appeal to me (some are too cartoony for my taste), there is an excellent volume devoted entirely to maps, several others with very stylish modern images, and useful artwork in the *Business & Industry* and *Design Elements* collections. I particularly like the new *Fabulous Fifties* assortment.

DYNAMIC GRAPHICS INC., 6000 North Forest Park Drive, Peoria, IL 61614; (800) 255-8800. A well-known publisher of traditional paper-based clip art, Dynamic Graphics offers a tremendous variety of stylish disk-based clip art in both bit-mapped and EPSF formats for both Macintosh and PC-compatible computers. Heavy clip-art users will want to consider building up their library by joining the company's Designer's Club, which provides a monthly shipment of new clip-art images.

Dynamic Graphics' clip-art has a clean, modern style that makes it distinctive.

MARKETING GRAPHICS INC. (MGI), 4401 Dominion Boulevard, Suite 210, Glen Allen, VA 23060; (804) 747-6991, (800) 368-3773. The businesslike *Publisher's PicturePaks* are available in bit-mapped, object-oriented, and EPSF formats for both IBM-compatible and Macintosh computers. The images are predominantly line art rather than heavily shaded illustrations, giving them a crisp, clean look and compatibility with many design styles.

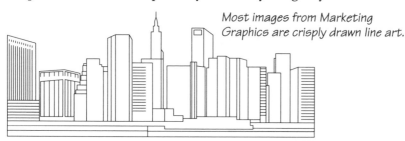

Most images from Marketing Graphics are crisply drawn line art.

Arts & Letters Editor provides thousands of illustrations like those above that can be used as provided, combined, and/or edited to achieve the desired effect.

A UNIQUE RESOURCE FOR PC-COMPATIBLE USERS

I have gotten a lot of mileage over the years from a hybrid computer illustration program/clip-art collection called *Arts & Letters Editor*, published by Computer Support Corporation, 15926 Midway Road, Dallas, TX 75244; (214) 661-8960.

On one hand, *Arts & Letters* is a powerful object-oriented drawing program that enables users to create freehand shapes, manipulate type, and create statistical charts. However, it also comes with a clip-art library of 5,000 symbols that can be combined, revised, twisted, and reshaped into an impressive variety of illustrations. Need an image of a skeleton, or a snowman, or a helicopter, or a road sign, or a spark plug, or an American flag, or a light bulb…the list goes on and on. *Arts & Letters* is a one-stop-shopping clip-art resource that constantly comes in handy.

A SPECIAL NOD TO DOVER BOOKS

A goldmine of clip art at very reasonable prices comes from Dover Publications. Their books run the gamut from old-time advertising artwork and typography to superb collections of animal illustrations, flowers, architectural renderings, ornate display alphabets, borders and frames…. Just leafing through their catalog is guaranteed to stimulate your imagination. And that catalog is free for the asking by writing to Dover Publications, 31 East 2nd St., Mineola, NY 11501.

These Dover clip-art images, scanned at 300 dpi, are typical in their fine detail and excellent quality.

SCAN? YES YOU CAN!

Of course, if you're going to work with paper-based clip art, either from Dover Publications books or from other copyright-free sources, you're going to need a way to incorporate them in your publication. As mentioned above, you can simply hand the original over to the print shop and have them reproduce the illustration using traditional means. But it is often simpler and less expensive to use an image scanner.

Image scanners can also be used to incorporate photographs into your laser-printed publication. The reproduction quality won't be "photographic," but if you make the right decisions in the scanning process it will be adequate for a variety of purposes.

We discussed the capabilities of scanners in Chapter 2. Now let's delve into ways to make the most of this sometimes finicky piece of equipment.

Using a scanner to grab an image from a piece of paper and move it into the computer is the kind of quirky process that makes otherwise rational people hurl epithets, blasphemy, and miscellaneous foul slanders at their innocent collection of chips and circuit boards.

No, the machine is not purposely fouling up your scan, no matter how certain you are that the hard disk just chuckled malevolently in your direction. You are merely facing the formidable combination of mumbo jumbo and trial-and-error that afflicts the scanning process. Spend a few minutes with me here and we'll cut the mumbo jumbo down to size and eliminate a few of the errors in the inevitable trial-and-error process.

Those Troublesome Gray Areas

I think most people "get" the basics of straight black-and-white scanning technology. The scanner looks at your picture and sees a black dot where the picture is dark and a white dot where the picture is light. When it comes time to reproduce that scanned picture on your system printer, the computer re-creates the image by ordering up dots of black toner on white paper. In this scheme the concept of "resolution" is no problem — if you have a 300-dpi laser printer, you scan the image at the 300-dpi setting and you're all set.

The veil of mumbo jumbo descends upon us when we venture

into the world of grayscale scanning. But the first step in understanding grayscale scanning is simple enough. Instead of recording each area in your original image as black or white, the scanner sees it as a shade of gray. The current crop of scanners can distinguish 256 shades of gray, which is just about the number of shades that the human eye can distinguish.

Just because your eye can see that many shades, though, doesn't mean your printer can reproduce them. Laser printers and even high-resolution imagesetters can only produce black dots. To create the illusion of gray, they group those dots into patterns. That's why it doesn't pay to scan a grayscale image at the 300-dpi resolution setting of your scanner — a laser printer will have to use several dots to represent each gray level, so much of that information you scanned will simply be wasted. What's worse, you'll slow down the printing process and have a file that eats up several megabytes of hard disk space.

What settings for gray levels and resolution should you use, then? For 300-dpi laser printing, 16 levels of gray at 70- to 80-dpi resolution is the practical maximum. If you're planning to send your scanned image out for high-resolution imagesetter output, use as many gray levels as your scanner will provide, but there's still no sense scanning at more than 150-dpi resolution. The only significant exception to these guidelines comes when you're planning to greatly enlarge your scanned image, in which case you should boost the resolution setting.

The Advantages of Grayscale

With the conceptual stuff behind us, we're ready to answer the most significant question about grayscale scanning: Why bother? In a word, the answer is flexibility.

Scanning in black and white produces a fixed pattern of dots. If you then try to change the size of the scanned image, you either crunch those dots together, which often produces blotches and distracting patterns, or pull them apart, reducing the sharpness of the image. When you work with grayscale images, the black-and-white dot pattern is created from the gray level information at print time, after you have sized the picture. That means you'll get a uniform, accurate dot pattern in your printout.

Editing the scanned image is also easier and more effective when working with grayscale images rather than a fixed dot pattern. For example, I was recently working with a Logitech 256 grayscale hand-held scanner and the *Ansel* image-editing software that comes with it. My initial scan looked fairly crummy — not a great surprise, considering that the original photo was not the best. However, I was able to tweak the brightness and contrast of the image to achieve a better-looking balance. I then used the software's Sharpen function to make the image crisper. To eliminate small distracting elements in the picture, I selected a gray value from the background and "painted over" the parts I didn't want. Finally, I used the Equalize command, a sophisticated tool that makes the lightest shade in the picture white, the darkest shade black, and adjusts the rest of the gray shades in the picture to create a more pleasing range of tones. By the time I was done (and it didn't take more than half an hour), my scanned reproduction looked a heck of a lot better than the original photograph.

TIPS AND SHORTCUTS

As I mentioned earlier, the scanning process inevitably involves a certain amount of trial and error. The best combination of settings will vary from image to image depending on the original's contrast and darkness, level of detail, colors, and (I've always suspected) the phases of the moon. However, the following tips should improve your success rate, and cut down on the time it takes you to get there.

Watch Those Horizontals!

The biggest problem in scanning line art is aligning the horizontal lines so they're perfectly parallel with the scanner head. If they're off by even a tiny fraction, you'll get the dreaded stairstep effect in your scan.

There is no foolproof workaround to this problem. If you're using a hand-held scanner, you may gain more control by aligning a book or heavy straightedge along the vertical side of the paper you're scanning and using this as a guide.

A flatbed scanner makes it easier to tackle this problem, since you can adjust the position of the original after each attempt. One trick that has significantly improved my "hit ratio" with a flatbed scanner is to place the original face down on a light box (or a window with the sun streaming through it) and use a straightedge to draw a line from edge to edge on the back of the paper, following the horizontal in the illustration. I then align the ends of the line I drew with the ruler markings printed along the outer borders of the scanner glass.

Judge From a Printout, Not From Your Screen

No matter what kind of monitor you're using, it will provide at best a rough guesstimate of what your final printed output will look like. A 72-dpi Macintosh black-and-white monitor can't provide the detail of a 300-dpi printer. A color monitor on a PC or a Mac can produce screen dots in shades of gray, so your image will look better on-screen than it will on your black-and-white-only printer. Either way, a printed paper sample is the only reliable way to judge.

Try Scanning a Copy

Scanning color photographs or images sometimes produces unpleasant surprises. This is especially true when the color of the light used by your scanner is the same as an important color in the original picture. For example, many hand-held scanners use a red light, which helps enhance the contrast of a black-and-white scan. However, use a red-light scanner on a color portrait and the face, once merely ghostly, turns a whiter shade of pale.

In these circumstances, a good, sharp photocopy that turns medium-dark colors into shades of gray often produces a noticeably better scan. You may also want to work from a copy when your original image is too large for the scanner. Some scanner software lets you stitch together multiple scans into a larger image, but it's often easier to scan a reduced photocopy in the first place.

Scanning a Screened Image

If your original is a printed piece, it has probably already been screened — that is, broken up into a pattern of dots for printing purposes. When you scan an image composed of a pattern of dots, your computer adds its own pattern of dots and the result can be strange and interesting patterns called moirés — sometimes very attractive in a psychedelic kind of way, but probably not what you had in mind.

One way to avoid the problem is to shrink the original slightly while scanning. Another possibility is to reduce your scanning resolution. Either strategy will often eliminate the distinction between dots in the scanning process. If you are using a grayscale scanner, you can then enlarge the resulting scan with little loss of detail.

Another technique is to avoid adding another dot pattern to the image by scanning it not as a photograph, but as line art. This works especially well with relatively coarse images, such as newspaper photographs.

COPYRIGHTS AND WRONGS

The final, critically important point to keep in mind about scanning images is not technological but legal. Scanning hardware and software makes it easy to acquire and reproduce illustrations indiscriminately. But scan in haste, repent at leisure! Images you find in published sources are generally protected by copyright law, and copyright holders are becoming increasingly vigilant in clamping down on unauthorized use of their visual property. Use clip-art books. Use original photos and artwork. Buy a photo from a stock house that sells reproduction rights to their images. But don't help yourself to printed pictures without first clearing reproduction rights with the copyright holder.

CHARTS AND GRAPHS

There's text, which conveys information through description. And there are pictures, which convey information visually. And then there are charts and graphs, which take information that might ordinarily be delivered via text and turn it into a visual statement.

As a computer-based publisher, you have a wide selection of software available for creating attractive charts and graphs with no manual dexterity required. Most spreadsheets offer graphing facilities, complete with the ability to export the result in a format your page-layout program can import.

If you rely on charts and graphs extensively, you might want to

Charts and graphs give dry statistics visual impact. This 3-dimensional chart was prepared using DeltaGraph.

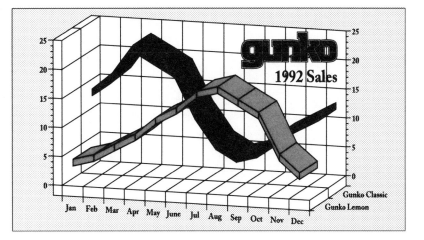

invest in one of the special-purpose tools dedicated to this purpose. Programs such as *Harvard Graphics* (from Software Publishing Corp.) for MS-DOS systems and *DeltaGraph* (from DeltaPoint Software) for the Macintosh are highly flexible and powerful systems for turning numbers into images.

My purpose here isn't to review the multitude of software available for the purpose of creating charts and graphs (that subject alone could fill a book) but to suggest ten ways you can use these graphic devices to communicate more effectively.

1. Give Your Statistics Visual Impact

Numbers presented in statistical form are just numbers. Readers have to flex their imaginations to give those figures size and proportion. Creating a chart or graph that visually represents the quantities involved gives them a handy shortcut for the process of translating statistical data into information with impact.

The mistake I see too often, though, is asking the reader to draw too much hard data from the visual representation. If you simply want to convey a sense of size or direction of a trend, you can go light on the labeling and captioning. However, if the audience is expected to pull actual figures from your publication, don't be afraid of redundancy. Label both the axes of a graph and the individual points plotted. Include the figures cited in a caption, or the accompanying text. Go out of your way to make it easy to both see the visualized representation of the data and pull out the data used to generate that representation, if that level of detail is important to your readers.

2. Summarize

In a lengthy publication, your data may be scattered over the course of many pages. Instead of asking your readers to remember the statistics dropped like breadcrumbs along the path, make their life easier by bringing the data together periodically in summary charts.

3. Provide Information at a Glance

You may create a publication from front to back and page by page, but it's a rare reader who approaches the end result that way. Most of us thumb through a document first, scanning to get a sense of the task to come and deciding whether to bother reading it at all. Graphs and charts can effectively capture that pre-reader's attention, boldly making a statement and delivering instant info.

And even for the dedicated reader, meaningful charts and graphs serve as excellent keys to retaining information.

4. Pictorialize Numerical Information

What was that last figure again? Was that 7,452 head of cattle or heads of lettuce? Did you sell 300 jars of Jane's Homemade Jams and Jellies in 30 days, or 30 jars in 300 days?

Creating charts and graphs using pictorial representations of the data is a good way to tie figures to the physical items they represent in the mind of the reader. *USA Today* has become famous (or perhaps infamous?) for its regular use of pictograms, though it's a frequent ploy in many news and business magazines too. If you want to create a chart showing housing starts, stack little pictures of houses to appropriate levels. Did I hear somebody say that's corny? I make no excuses — it works.

5. Compare and Contrast

How did we do this year compared to last year? How does our income from mail order stack up against our income from over-the-counter retail sales? How do our costs of raw materials versus profit figures contrast over the product line? Visualizing this kind of information, which may develop over time or span a variety of sources, is an excellent use of charts and graphs.

One trick to making them work effectively in this instance is to choose the right scale to represent the figures involved. For instance, say the purpose of your chart is to demonstrate the monthly fluctuation in sales of Jane's Homemade Brownies, and the figures range between 4,000 and 5,000 units a month. The way to focus on the fluctuation is to lop off the bottom end of the scale (set the baseline to 3,000, for instance) and let each additional 1,000 brownies represent a substantial vertical distance.

6. Add Graphic Interest

What if you want to add illustrations to an all-text publication but there just aren't any pictures or pertinent artwork to be had? Charts and graphs can add visual pizzazz and excitement at virtually no expense. Keep them simple and bold, and consider graphic devices like gradient fills (where a shade changes smoothly from dark to light or vice versa) or even a second color to enhance the illustrative effect.

7. Tie a Publication Together

A nice touch for any publication is to include a recurring graphic element that ties the whole thing together. Often it's a decorative border, or a distinctive treatment for the page numbers. But if statistics are an important part of your subject, why not use a graphical representation of those numbers as your recurring visual device?

For example, say you're preparing a 24-page booklet about the six activities your nonprofit organization undertakes. Create a six-part labeled pie chart. Then create six versions, each with a different section "exploded" (pulled away from the main circle), and run the version of the pie chart appropriate to the activity you're discussing in a wide margin alongside the text. This provides a ready reference to the overall statistical picture, a handy index for browsers, and a consistent graphic that unifies the publication. Not a bad set of benefits from a simple pie chart.

8. Organize Unwieldy Data

Sometimes straight text is a tough way to digest information. For instance, *Home Office Computing* frequently includes listings for a dozen or more products along with an article, with extensive product specifications and contact information. To make this wealth of data manageable, the magazine presents it in chart form (often prepared using the table feature in *Microsoft Word*). With information arrayed in rows and columns and ruling lines between them, readers can scan the listings easily and zero in on products appropriate to their computer systems, budgets, and individual needs.

9. Present Fluctuating Data

Many businesses prepare documents and publications with text that changes infrequently, if at all, but figures that must be kept up to date. Rather than incorporating the figures in the text, risking layout changes that ripple through the publication and the possibility that some figures might be missed in the updating process, present the data in a self-contained chart.

10. Create Presentation Elements

Do you prepare desktop-published materials that are then used as the basis for live presentation and discussion? If so, graphs and charts included in the published version can easily be reused as overhead projections or slides to punctuate the presentation. The visuals set the framework for discussion, the details are conveyed in the oral version, and the two come together for reinforcement and future reference in the printed material.

A Necessary Evil?

As far as I'm concerned, statistics are a necessary evil. I prefer adjectives. But even a numerophobe like myself has to admit that in a business setting, reporting that we sold a humongous quantity of Jane's Homemade Jam and a truly awe-inspiring number of brownies probably won't project an appropriate business image. Like it or not, I'm stuck with stats. At least I have computer-generated charts and graphs to make them substantially more palatable.

CHAPTER 7

Design That Works

We've discussed typography and illustration — the building blocks of your publication layout. Now it's time to put it all together into a design that conveys the desired impression.

Design is an art that can be intimidating. However, there are also basic practices, procedures, tips, and techniques that allow amateur desktop publishers to produce publications that are at the least acceptable and sometimes inspired. Getting a few of these "rules of thumb" under your belt is a good way to take the psychic curse off the design process.

WHY RULES OF THUMB?

When I set out to write about "rule-of-thumb" design guidelines I started wondering where the phrase "rule of thumb" came from in the first place. Turns out there are two schools of thought on the subject. One is based on the fact that a man's thumb is about 1 inch across, making it a handy tool for approximate measurement. The other hearkens back to the days when a brewmaster would check whether the fermentation process was proceeding properly by dipping his thumb into a batch of beer to judge its temperature.

I suppose the first derivation is more likely to be accurate, but the image of a thumb soaked in suds is closer to my purpose here. Like the brewer's art, publication design is rooted in hundreds of years of practice and tradition. Yet even with all that history and accumulated knowledge, we still don't have a "design thermometer" with precise degree markings to guide our typographic decisions. Instead, like the brewmaster, we rely on "rules of thumb" to get us within shooting distance of success, then submit our creation to a personal taste test to judge its ultimate success or failure.

Here are a few pointers to keep in mind.

Use a Comfortable Line Length

Type set in very narrow lines is tiresome to read — your eye has to jump back to the left edge of the column every few words. It tends to look pretty hideous too, with an overabundance of hyphenated words and inappropriate spaces.

What I see more often in desktop publishing projects, though, are lines that seem to go on forever. Getting through these wide-load columns is like asking your eyes to run the marathon: Readers are likely to stumble as they near the end of each line, lose their place in midparagraph, and just give up before reaching the finish line.

There is no hard-and-fast "optimal" line length, since the type size and design must be taken into account. However, there is a good rule-of-thumb guideline: most text faces work best when set with 55 to 60 characters (9 to 10 words) per line. You should generally set sans serif type in narrower columns than serif type.

Another common rule of thumb for setting the line length is to type out one and a half lowercase alphabets (a–z plus a–m) in a given typeface, measure the printed width, and take that as your standard. This method is more appropriate for a newsletter or magazine layout than a book or other single-column design.

Minimize Use of ALL CAPS

When all you had was a typewriter, hitting Shift Lock and banging away in all capitals was one of the few ways you could call attention to a really important piece of text. With desktop publishing we have better devices, including larger type sizes and bolder type weights. All-capital type, with all the letters the same height, tends to look squared-off and blocky. That makes it both unattractive and hard to read. All caps are OK for short, newspaper-style screaming headlines, but even then I'd try a bold typeface set in uppercase and lowercase in a large size instead.

Don't Underline

Here's another holdover from typewriter days. Underlining looks amateurish in a desktop-published piece. There just isn't any elegant position for an underline — if it fits close to the bottom of the letters it can touch or cut through the descenders (the tails of the "g," "q," "y," etc.). If it's low enough to clear the descenders, it's too far away from the word it's underscoring, and hovers perilously close to the line below. You can achieve the same kind of emphasis using italics or (sometimes) boldface type.

Avoid Long Italic Settings

Italics are often very attractive letterforms, with more swash and movement than the straight up-and-down ordinary version of a typeface. However, the way italics lean forward makes them fit together in a way that's hard to read in extended passages.

Italics are terrific for adding diversity to a layout when used in moderation, though. You'll often see italicized captions for illustrations, photographs, and charts. Introductory material is often set in italics — the editor's opening "blurb" before chapters in an anthology, for example, or the writer's introduction to the monthly *Playboy* Interview (honest, Mom, I only buy it for the typography).

Blocks of italics are also used frequently in setting the answer to a Letter to the Editor or to a question in a "Q&A" feature. I recently included a Q&A in a project and experimented with setting the answers in italics. Ultimately, though, I found it worked better to set the question section in bold and the answer in my regular text face. Lengthy blocks of italic type seemed to wash away on the page, while the contrast between bold and regular type gave a nice give-and-take, one-two punch to the piece.

Limit Your Type Selection

The easiest way to achieve type harmony is to limit the number of typefaces you employ in each project. Rule of thumb says no more than two. I say start out by trying just one.

Sound boring? It doesn't have to be, since each typeface gives you bold and italic styles to play with, and a choice of sizes. I especially like working with typefaces that offer more than a single bold weight. ITC Clearface, for example, comes in regular and regular italic, bold and bold italic, heavy and heavy italic, black and black italic. I can stick with Clearface for an entire newsletter, with nice chunky dark headlines, a second bold weight in a smaller size for secondary heads, a highly legible text face that fits plenty of characters per column inch, a handsome bold for text subheads, and an attractive italic for captions.

Use Contrasting Type

Wait a minute — I just said you should strive for type harmony. Doesn't contrast contradict that?

Not at all. I have a harmonious marriage; my wife and I are roughly the same types of people. But we also have contrasting areas in our personalities, abilities, and interests — that's what keeps things lively. And the same principle holds true in typography.

In the newsletter example above I achieve contrast with a typeface that features dramatically different levels of boldness and increase the effect by using significantly different type sizes in my headlines. Another common strategy is to use a typeface with serifs for basic text and a sans serif face for headlines and captions. Either way, the point is to create areas of darkness and light on the page, to create shapes that attract your reader's eye and encourage it to move around the page. Type selection goes hand in hand with design and illustration to produce this effect.

Get the Lead In!

Most desktop publishing programs have a setting that automatically adds space between lines of type (leading). Generally the leading automatically inserted by your page-layout program is 20 percent of

This newsletter was created using several different type styles and weights from the Clearface family. The same newsletter with different typography is shown on page 145.

the type height, conforming to another tried-and-true rule of thumb. It's a good place to start, but I'd urge you to experiment with this setting on your own and check out the results. The less space between lines, the darker the text block will appear. There will be times when you want that blacker impression to attract the reader's eye and can cut down on leading without sacrificing legibility.

On the other hand, adding more space between lines lightens up a block of text. If you use a relatively wide column, added leading makes the longer lines less intimidating and easier to read. You can also try setting discrete blocks of text with overly generous leading (about double, or even triple, the point size of the type) to achieve a quick-and-easy decorative effect in your layout. For example, you will sometimes find magazine layouts in which each article begins with the first paragraph set with double the leading of the body text in order to draw the reader's eye into the story.

When in Doubt, Ragged Right

Virtually any desktop publishing program lets you set justified type — that means it lines up at both the left and right margins (the way the text you're reading is set). To justify text, the program will add space between words (and sometimes between letters) and use hyphens to break words between lines.

The alternative is to align the left side and let lines end on the right side where the words logically break, which is called *ragged right*. Justified text can have its advantages. It looks more formal and imposes a sense of rectangular order on the page. Whenever I can, though, I stick with ragged right.

This is a choice based on both aesthetics and convenience. Aesthetically, ragged-right type has the same amount of space between each word, so the lines of type look smooth and even on the page. In terms of convenience, justified setting requires you spend a lot more time policing the choices made by your page-layout program. Did it put hyphens in acceptable places? Are there too many hyphenated lines one after another? Did some of the lines require too much spacing to fit the full column width? This intensive checking and manual adjustment is eliminated if you go with a ragged-right setting.

Which doesn't mean you should abandon hyphenation entirely when setting ragged right. You want the right edge of the text to ripple gently down the page. If there are unsightly gaps, you'll have to get in there and hyphenate to even things out.

Experiment!

I'm always impressed with the way a professional designer can mentally visualize a page layout. I don't have that ability. But I do have a few rules of thumb to guide me in the right direction, and a desktop publishing system that lets me quickly try out a variety of typographic options and judge their effectiveness based on actual printouts. With this combination of basic knowledge and computer technology, even those of us without formal training can produce attractive publications.

DESKTOP PUBLISHING POWER FEATURES

When I worked as a computerless book editor, asking to wrap text around an irregularly shaped image was asking for trouble. It involved somebody in the art department giving detailed instructions

AWAY
AWAY

VOW
VOW

The words above are shown without manual kerning on top, and with kerning adjustments below. The differences are subtle, but add professionalism to your headline typesetting.

for the wrap to a typesetter, paying substantially extra for the custom work, and rarely having it come out right the first time. More time, more money, more aggravation. The heck with it, let's just use rectangular pictures.

Now, with desktop publishing, a host of interesting design features are at my disposal. For example, when I want to wrap text around a graphic, I scan in the image, see picture and text on my screen, make the necessary adjustments, and quickly print working proofs on a laser printer till it all lines up just right.

The same holds true for many other effects that used to involve time-consuming hand labor, such as beginning a story with an over-sized capital letter, placing a highlighted block of text in a drop-shadowed box, and using solid or tinted bars to add shape to a layout. Desktop publishing software gives you the power to add spice to a design. And unless you're a lot more jaded than I am, using that power is frankly fun. The trick is knowing how to use these powerful features to create more effective layouts, and not just to show off the neat tricks you can accomplish with your computer.

Let's examine a few of the design elements you can create with even moderately powerful desktop publishing software, with some tips on the role these elements play in good design and hints on making your version of these effects look as good as the traditional professional variety.

KERNING AND TRACKING

"Kerning" and "tracking" are both terms for controlling the spacing between letters. Tracking is the space consistently placed between individual letters in a block of text. You may not find the term in your page-layout program manual; adjusting this spacing is sometimes referred to as "condensed" and "expanded" spacing, or sometimes lumped in under kerning.

More accurately, though, kerning refers to spacing between pairs of letters whose shapes leave unsightly gaps unless they're tucked closer together. For example, look closely at the way the letters "A" and "T" stand next to each other. Placing the left edge of the top of the "T" to the right of the bottom serif of the "A" leaves an awful lot of white space — the letters don't seem to hold together properly. To solve this graphic flaw you can kern the letters — moving them closer so the "A" tucks under the top of the "T." Some of the other letter pairs that typically require kerning include "AW," "Av," "OX," "Vo," and "xc" — and there are many more.

Tracking and kerning information are built into computer typefaces. For body text, these default values are usually good enough, though you may want to experiment with modest adjustments. If you need to squeeze a slightly higher character count into a block of text, for instance, tracking the text a little tighter may accomplish this goal without hurting the look of the setting. The success or failure of this strategy will depend on the specific font design.

When it comes to setting larger type for headlines, you should definitely take time to adjust the letterspacing manually. The kerning values built into computerized typefaces are usually adequate for body text, but large-size type often requires additional attention, and leaving gaps and uncomfortably close positionings in headline type are clear indications that the type was set by an amateur.

Letterspacing your type is not simply a mechanical process. It involves an aesthetic judgment. Type that's set very tight sends a graphic message: It appears darker and more urgent. Take a close look at the display type in magazine ads and book jackets and you'll often find it set "TNT" — tight but not touching. Overdo the effect, though, and readability suffers; the text may appear intimidating.

Judging whether text is properly kerned when you're reading it can be tricky — the meaning of the words influences the way you perceive them. That's why I like a tip offered by Adobe in their *Font & Function* type catalog: "Try looking at your text while it's turned sideways or upside down." Unsuspecting onlookers may think you've lost your marbles, but it works.

A final note about this and any other task where you're judging spacing with a critical eye: Rely on a printed proof and not on the image you see on screen. Your printer has much higher resolution than your monitor, and the differences in spacing between the two can be striking.

INITIAL CAPS

There's nothing new about using oversized capital letters as a design technique. The medieval scribes used extravagantly beautiful miniature paintings to ornament the first letter of sections of text in their

Lorem ipsum dolor sit amet, consectetuer adipiscing elit, sed diam nonummy nibh euismod tincidunt ut laoreet dolore magna aliquam erat volutpat. Ut wisi enim ad minim veniam, quis nostrud exerci tation ullamcorper suscipit lobortis

Lorem ipsum dolor sit amet, consectetuer adipiscing elit, sed diam nonummy nibh euismod tincidunt ut laoreet dolore magna aliquam erat volutpat. Ut wisi enim ad minim veniam, quis nostrud exerci tation ullamcorper suscipit lobortis nisl ut aliquip ex ea commodo consequat. Duis autem vel eum iriure

The setting on the left has a raised cap; at right is a drop cap. Raised caps add more white space to your layout, while drop caps use space more economically.

illuminated manuscripts. Incorporating large initial capitals in more mundane publications is still a wonderful way to break up copy-heavy material with bright visual highlights.

Initial caps use typography itself as illustration. They are also functional, leading the reader's eye directly to the beginning of a section.

You will sometimes see initial caps positioned with their bottom aligned with the baseline of the first line of text and their top in the air (called a *raised* cap). Often they are handled more elegantly by cutting them into the text, indenting several lines from the left margin and tucking in the oversized letter. This treatment is referred to as a *drop* cap.

Although the safest type choice for an initial cap is a larger-size version of the body face (usually the height of three lines of body text and sometimes bold), this is not an ironclad rule. You might, for instance, use a sans serif initial cap in a serif text setting (particularly if you are using sans serif headline type). If you do use a different face for your initial caps, however, make sure it provides a major contrast to the text face.

A potential highlight for initial capitals is printing them in color. This may draw too much attention in a sparsely illustrated publication but works well in a layout with other, colorful artwork.

Still another possibility hearkens back to medieval days by using illustrated letters. There are many striking copyright-free examples of illustrated letters available in clip-art books and disk-based clip-art collections.

A few high-end desktop software programs (such as *Ventura Publisher*) will handle placement of drop caps automatically, but most page-layout programs require you to adjust the positioning manually. There are three key alignment points to watch.

The initial cap must always hit the left margin, and the bottom must line up with the baseline of the appropriate line of text (first line for raised caps, the appropriate indented line for drop caps).

Drop caps sometimes extend above the level of the surrounding copy. When they do, they need to be large enough so it's clear the effect was intentional, and not merely a failure to line up the top of the drop cap with the top of the first text line.

Avoid leaving excessive gaps between the body text and the shape of the initial cap. If the letter has a slanted side ("A," "V," "W," etc.), adjust each line of body text horizontally to leave a consistent space between the side of the initial cap and the beginning of the text line. There is an exception to this rule: If the letter is a word in itself (the article "A," or a letter being used as a word), then leave its rectangular space alone.

THE STRAIGHT AND NARROW

Sometimes the shortest distance between a confused layout and a well-composed page is a straight line.

Lines used as graphic elements in a layout are usually referred to as rules. Their thickness is measured using points (the same units we use to measure type height). A 2-point rule is a fairly thick line; a very thin line, usually called a hairline, is a ¼-point rule.

If you're printing drafts using a laser printer and having the final page layouts output on professional typesetting equipment, watch out for your hairline rules. The typesetter can print much finer lines than your laser printer. That means that the "hairline" rule you print at 300 dpi can be much thicker than the one you get back from the typesetter. Ask to see a sample before you have your entire job set, and adjust the point-size specification of your rules if necessary.

Column Rules

Why use thin vertical rules between columns? One answer is purely practical: You can position columns of type closer together if you run a thin vertical rule between them, thus fitting more material on a page. In the main news section, for example, *The New York Times* runs six columns across with barely more than half a pica between columns. That's very tight. If there were no hairline rules between columns, your eye would jump right across that thin intercolumn spacing and the newspaper would be virtually unreadable. In the business section, on the other hand, "All the News That's Fit to Print" fits into a five-column grid with more space between columns, so the intercolumn rules are eliminated.

Even if you can allow more generous space between columns, you may like the way a hairline column rule organizes the page for your readers. *Newsweek*, for instance, runs intercolumn hairlines even with a full pica between columns, and the result is an easy flow of the reader's eye through the text. Illustrations frequently break up the ruling lines, keeping them from becoming oppressively consistent. And short ruling lines, the same weight as the intercolumn rule, are used to separate captions from body text and subheads from major headings and body text. Using a consistently weighted rule in several places helps tie the whole page together. The ruled editorial pages are also clearly distinguished from the ad pages surrounding them.

In my own projects, I am a big fan of setting type ragged right instead of justifying it. Sometimes, though, a ragged right setting needs organizational help — text blocks with varying line lengths can seem to float in space. Adding hairline column rules lets me compromise, imposing organization without slowing down the typesetting operation.

Horizontal Rules

Using horizontal rules can both separate individual sections of your text and help hold your design together with repeated visual elements.

For example, you will generally want to be visually consistent in defining the tops and bottoms of your pages. With a novel or other straight-text setting that's not very difficult — just use the same number of lines per page. But what if your text breaks up logically into lots of separate sections of different lengths? Suppose you were creating a company phone directory with a page or two per letter, or a "Field Guide to Wild Snarks" with a photo and species description of varying length on each page? You could use bold running headers and footers to hold the tops and bottoms, but you can also use horizontal rules to establish your territory while allowing a varied layout from page to page. Often the two strategies are used together by creating headers and footers that include horizontal rules.

Horizontal rules also work well if your text breaks into many separate subsections. I recently picked up the government form to apply for a Social Security number. The instructions are neatly broken up into eleven bite-sized sections. Each person dealing with these instructions will need to refer to only a few of these items. For example, there's a paragraph headed "IF YOU HAVE NEVER HAD A SOCIAL SECURITY NUMBER," another, "IF YOU NEED TO REPLACE YOUR CARD," and still another, "IF YOU NEED TO CHANGE YOUR NAME ON YOUR CARD." The designer came up with an elegant solution. The 8 ½-inch width is divided into a narrow (12-pica) left column for subheads and a wider (30-pica) column for explanatory text. The horizontal rule between sections incorporates two widths, thicker above the narrow column, then thinner across to the left margin.

The result may not win any design awards, but it's a good functional layout, clear, browsable, and unintimidating. The rules both separate the page vertically and tie the two columns together horizontally. A similar strategy works well for product brochures, seminar listings, and other material where the reader will pick and choose items of interest. I have also seen thin horizontal rules used very effectively to separate the sections of a résumé.

Horizontal rules can also be used for headline treatment and to highlight a pull quote.

Headline Treatment

The different departments within a publication might be consistently set with a ruling line above and below for easy identification.

A horizontal rule can also serve as a background for dropped-out heading type. Printing white letters on a thick black rule, for example, when used sparingly, will immediately draw the reader's eye. This technique is especially helpful when you need emphasis but don't have room to use a large typeface.

Horizontal rules of different widths separate this page vertically, but tie the two columns together horizontally. This design strategy works well for brochures, listings, and other material where the reader will pick and choose.

Highlighting a Pull Quote

A pull quote is a short, intriguing excerpt from the main text, set large in a separate block as a sort of appetizer. Pull quotes are sometimes boxed but often look better with rules top and bottom to distinguish them from the surrounding text without imprisoning them completely. You may want to use a decorative line treatment here, such as a scotch rule (a thin and a thick rule used together).

BOXES

Boxing a block of text gives it a separate identity. This works well when creating a sidebar — copy that relates to the main story but is not essential reading. Typical sidebars are glossary items, additional information about a specific point in the main text, or a listing of technical specifications.

Since the boxed text is a separate element, you will probably want to include a heading or subheading to define its purpose.

Illustrations can also benefit from being boxed. If the graphic already has well-defined corners, such as a photograph, then adding a box is usually overkill. Sometimes the shape of the graphic leaves it floating in a sea of white space, though; maps are a typical example here. By enclosing the graphic in a ruled box your page looks neater, and you can also neatly enclose legends and caption material.

TEXT WRAPS

When you played with blocks as a kid, you probably didn't just stack same-size rectangles on top of one another. Instead you played around with different shapes and sizes, trying for interesting patterns while maintaining balance. Designing pages is basically a two-dimensional version of the same game. And wrapping text around graphics lets you experiment with lots of new shapes.

You can wrap text around rectangular graphics or be adventurous and make lines of text break around the edges of an irregularly shaped graphic. In either case, be sure to maintain a consistent gap between text and graphics throughout your project.

The pitfall in wrapping text around graphics is sacrificing legibility. That's why I generally avoid breaking the right edge of a text column — it serves as the consistent anchor as the reader scans the page. An irregular left side is less of a reading problem, as long as you maintain a reasonable number of words on each line. If the text lines become very short, you're demanding too much jumping around for the privilege of reading your deathless prose. You're also asking for typesetting problems of excessive spacing and hyphenation, particularly in justified settings.

THE DOWNSIDE OF GRAPHIC DEVICES

I know of only one advantage that manual techniques for creating publications have over using desktop publishing software. The traditional approach makes you stop and think.

Do you want to put six different blocks of text in boxes on the page? The person who has to draw each of those boxes by hand might have a very different answer from the computer user. How about putting vertical lines between columns of text? For many desktop publishing users this is as simple as making a single menu choice — but does that make it a good idea?

The most common complaint about desktop-published documents is their busyness. The ease of creating graphic devices using page-layout software often leads to "too much of a good thing." Adding boxes and borders and eating up white space with text wraps can darken your pages, making them dense and uninviting. And asking the reader's eye to focus on too many competing graphic highlights on a page is worse than simply reading straight text.

Fortunately, desktop publishing software lets you experiment to your heart's content. Take the extra couple of minutes to add a few graphic flourishes to your page and examine the printed proof with a critical eye. Even if the result doesn't quite work for your current project, you may be able to use the same device at a later date.

But proceed with a sense of restraint. When it comes to adding graphic elements to your page layouts, you literally have to know when to draw the line.

TEMPLATES: PREPACKAGED DESIGN TOOLS

I'd be the last person to deny the sensory and psychological satisfactions of cooking a meal from scratch. Measuring and sifting, grating and mixing, producing seductive smells and fascinating textures...the heck with writing this chapter, I'm going downstairs to make some brownies!

Ah, but there's the rub. How often does a home-based entrepreneur like me have time to start cooking from scratch? My freezer is stocked full of frozen shortcuts. In fact, if my accountant weren't so conservative, I'd be inclined to try deducting the microwave oven as a business expense. After all, the more time I spend in the kitchen, the less time in my home office.

Templates are the desktop publishing equivalent of prepackaged foods. They are prepared publication pages, fully laid out with dummy text instead of actual articles and placeholders filling in for graphics. They may not have quite as much spice and subtlety as layouts prepared from scratch, but they offer three distinct advantages: speed, design guidance, and consistency.

Speed

With the basic layout and type styles set, building a page using templates is a fill-in-the-blanks procedure. However, you can't just

Templates like these from (left to right) Personal Press, Publish It!, and Express Publisher provide helpful design shortcuts for novices and a good jumping-off point even for experienced desktop publishers.

set your brain on cruise control; tailoring your copy and graphics to suit the template requires care and creativity. Still, using a template with the basic page elements in place, the columns and ruling guides structured, the running heads and/or feet already positioned, the typefaces selected and sized, and a multiplicity of mundane matters already managed will cut down on production time significantly.

Design Guidance

The templates I have seen tend toward good, solid workmanlike layout, forsaking flash for the sake of broad applicability. If you are unsure of your design sense, or even the rules guiding design decisions, a professionally prepared template is a wonderful place to start. For most jobs, "workmanlike" is perfectly acceptable, and usually a lot better than what an inexperienced designer might concoct when working from the blank page up.

Consistency

One of the first signs of amateurish desktop publishing is inconsistency from page to page or issue to issue. Through ignorance or carelessness, the desktop duffer uses different margins on different pages. There are hairline rules separating columns of text on page 2 and not on page 4. There is a wide gap separating the picture from its caption on page 1 and barely a hair's breadth left between the picture and caption on page 5. Major headlines are all capital letters one month, upper and lower case the next. The list goes on ad nauseam, but the net effect is a very poor impression. I'd rather see a mediocre design executed consistently than a layout with some eye-catching elements but a general disregard for uniformity. A template imposes structure, so you really have to go out of your way to muck it up.

You may have a stock of templates at your disposal already in the form of sample files included with your desktop publishing software package. And additional template packages for several programs are due to reach the market shortly. In addition, you will find publication templates widely available on desktop-publishing-oriented electronic bulletin boards, which you access through a modem.

Once you have your templates, how should you work with them? Here are some Do's and Don'ts to guide you.

DO Choose a Template With Care

Will it suit your specific text and graphic requirements? Better figure it out before you start building your publication than try to kludge your way out of a problem later.

For example, a two-column format may be fine if you are using horizontal graphics, but won't work well for vertical graphics such as the typical "head shot" portrait. On the other hand, the more columns you have, the more time you'll spend worrying about where paragraphs break and how items are positioned. A two-column layout saves time and should accommodate more text than a layout with more columns and more blank space between columns.

DON'T Be Too Proud to Use Times and Helvetica

The typical template uses these two typefaces or their generically named equivalents (Times is often called Dutch and Helvetica called Swiss). These faces are available on virtually any laser printer. They're built in to all the Apple LaserWriters (even older models) and are often bundled with PC-compatible desktop publishing software for the Hewlett-Packard LaserJet and compatibles.

There's another reason for the popularity of Times and Helvetica: they have been designed well for the 300-dpi resolution of the typical laser printer. Many typefaces that look wonderful when output on professional typesetting equipment look jagged and unappealing at 300 dpi. Sticking to old reliable Times and Helvetica solves that potential problem. Desktop publishing cognoscenti may snicker at these familiar typeface choices, but these old reliables will get the job done.

DON'T Be Afraid to Experiment

Having praised Times and Helvetica, let me encourage you to try the other available fonts when you have the time to experiment. The advantage to working with a template here is that you can quickly remake an entire publication with a new selection of typefaces and base your design decision on an actual printout.

To make this a successful exercise, use controlled experimentation. If the template uses sans serif headline type, try different sans serif typefaces for headlines rather than switching to a serif face. Also maintain the distinction between bold and italic faces presented by the template designer. And stick with the body-text justification used in the original template. There is a major design difference between the look of justified text and ragged-right text. In the latter case, hairline rules between columns, boxes, or other devices are sometimes used to neaten up the appearance of the page — devices that would be overkill with most justified-text settings. Let your template be your guide.

One more note about altering typefaces: Be sure to make changes consistently. If the original template uses variations of the body text face for subheads, captions, footnotes, page numbers, and so forth, be sure to change all these elements to the appropriate variation of the body text face you have chosen.

DO Master Your Page-Layout Program

It may seem easy to simply substitute your own text and graphics for template placeholders, but you will still need to know how to adjust column lengths, alter hyphenation, crop and size graphics, cut and paste elements, and so on.

DO Prepare a Character Count for Template Text Blocks

If you know the amount of space available in advance, you can edit to fit in your word processor where the process is relatively simple. Page-layout programs are notoriously slow and clumsy when it comes to major text editing.

Many word processors will count the characters in a story for you automatically. If yours doesn't, you can get a reasonable approximation by counting lines and multiplying by the average number of characters per line.

DON'T Force Copy to Fit by Making Major Typeface Changes

Switching from an 11-point type with 12 points of leading to 10-point type with 11 points of leading may not seem like a big deal mathematically, but it can drastically alter the look of a publication. The text blocks appear darker and more forbidding, and the proportion between body text and headline type is thrown off. Good design is a balancing act, and a professionally prepared template should maintain a pleasing equilibrium between white space, graphic elements, and the various text blocks. Tamper with that balance at your peril.

DO Protect Your Template Files

The best protection for any file is a backup copy, and you should certainly maintain at least two backups of the template files you use on separate floppy disks.

It is also a good idea to protect your template files at the operating system level. For DOS users, the attribute (ATTRIB) command lets you set the status of a file to "read only." That means you won't be able to change the file without going back to DOS and changing the attribute again. See your DOS manual for details. Macintosh users can lock a file by clicking the appropriate box in the Get Info window. You can make entire floppy disks read-only by covering a 5.25-inch disk's side notch or flipping the tab on a 3.5-inch disk.

DO Make Your Own Templates

When you have achieved a design you find pleasing, create a template version of it for future editions of the same publication or future projects with similar design requirements. It is a good idea to use nonsense text and blank frames for graphic placeholders in your template instead of simply saving off a copy of a completed page. That way, when you start "filling in the blanks" in your template in the future, the text blocks and graphics you have not already updated will be easier to spot.

DO Consider Commissioning a Template Design

If you are undertaking an ongoing project — a series of newsletters, for example, or a space ad that will appear regularly with different text — consider the one-time investment in a template created by a professional designer to your specifications. The one-time expense involved in bringing in a pro to establish the basic framework of your publication can be repaid many times over in the form of a more effective business communication tool. Make it clear to the designer up front that you want a templated design, though, and not just the layout for a one-shot publication. A good designer who understands your plans will produce a flexible template that provides for design diversity in the future and doesn't rely on characteristics unique to a single issue's content for its impact.

A Bonus Tip

Since you've saved loads of time using templates in your desktop publishing projects, I have one final hint to share. When making brownies, add a little brewed coffee to the recipe. It's a subtle change, I grant you, but my family like them that way.

NEED DESIGN INSPIRATION? LOOK AROUND YOU!

When it comes to producing a desktop publishing project, we often want what those design professionals possess: the ability to capture the reader's attention and generate excitement through layout and design.

So how are we going to get it? You could buy it, of course. I know

A type gauge (shown reduced here) lets you measure type size and leading, rule width, and more.

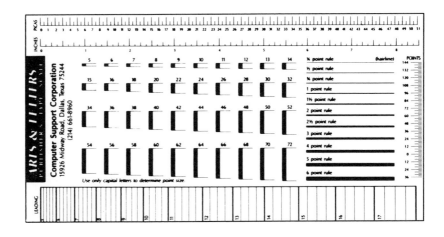

some really good designers who could use an extra client or two. Ah, but that involves a budget for art direction — a budget that's often missing in the world of one-person-does-it-all desktop publishing. So we'll do the next best thing — we'll borrow it.

The fact is, design ideas are borrowed all the time, and professional designers are the biggest culprits. How do you think new styles and trends in graphic design arise? One designer looks at somebody else's work and says, "Hey, this is a cool idea! I can use it for that Terwilliger Industries job," or words to that effect.

And if borrowing design ideas is good enough for professional designers, it's good enough for you and me.

TOOLS OF THE TRADE

There are only two absolutely essential tools for the budding borrower: a plastic type gauge and a supply of type catalogs.

The type gauge is available for a few dollars at most art supply stores. It's transparent, with separate areas for measuring the type size and line leading (the vertical distance between lines of type). There's usually a pica and/or inch ruler along the edge as well.

By aligning the plastic gauge over a layout you find attractive, you can read off the "vital statistics" of the type used. Pulling a nice, airy newsletter from my samples file and analyzing it with a type gauge, I find there are 3 columns, each 15 picas wide, with 2 picas between the columns). The body text is set in 10-point type with 12-point leading, the main headlines are set in 36-point type and the subheads are 18 point.

Ah, but what kind of type is it? That's where type catalogs come in handy. Many type publishers provide catalogs free; others charge a nominal sum. In either case it's a small price to pay to build a reference library of raw materials for design. If you're willing to spend a bit more, there are several reference books on the market that provide a sampling of type offerings from various publishers. *The LaserJet Font Book* and *The Macintosh Font Book*, both published by Peachpit Press, are two collections I find handy.

How do you identify the type used in a printed sample from literally thousands of suspects? Focus on the letters that are most distinctly different from typeface to typeface. For example, look at the letter "k." Do the two short lines meet in a V shape at the vertical bar, or do they intersect to the right of the bar? Similarly, look at the way the center point is formed in the letter "w." The shape of the lowercase "a" is often a good typeface fingerprint, and so is "g" in both the uppercase and the lowercase.

If the typeface has serifs, examine them carefully and note their shape. Whether or not there are serifs, check out the thickness of the lines that make up the letters and, very important, the difference between the thickest parts and the thinnest parts of the letters.

You may hit a perfect match by going through this kind of analytical exercise. Then again, you might not. In fact, even with hundreds of typefaces now available in computer-ready form, there are still thousands that simply are not available for personal computer use. However, in virtually any design, you can come up with a match that is close enough to reproduce the design effect you're after.

If you're planning to re-create some of the fancy headline type treatments you see in professional graphic layouts, you'll need an additional item in your set of tools — type-manipulation software, as described in Chapter 5. These are programs that let you distort and rearrange standard typestyles to make a graphic statement — adding perspective, squashing or stretching letter shapes, adding screened backgrounds or colors, and so on.

One final tool: a photocopying machine. On one hand this has an obvious use: to keep copies of attractive layouts for your file if you can't keep the publications where you found them. The other important use is sizing up the effectiveness of color layouts when rendered in black and white. Sometimes it's tough knowing what element of a layout is drawing your attention — successful use of color, or interesting typography and layout. If you're working on a black-and-white project, you can separate out the elements by making a photocopy of a color layout you're considering as source material and evaluating the copy.

Casing the Joint

Before we can grab the graphic loot and scoot, we have to figure out what's worth borrowing. This will vary depending on the type of project you're undertaking.

For books and newsletters, we're generally talking about structural issues — the basic type combination, the column layout, the size and placement of subheads, the treatment of running headers and footers. In addition, you may find distinctive graphic devices that strike your fancy.

A nice treatment of chapter openers or the running headers in a book layout may be ideas to borrow. In preparing this book layout, I looked at several books on my shelf in which the body text is set in a column significantly narrower than full-page width with a second, separate column for spot illustration and parenthetical asides. It worked for me.

When it comes to magazine layouts, handbills, and flyers, I often go hunting for interesting display-type treatments. Let's face it — unless I have the budget to hire a top-notch illustrator or photographer, there's no way I can borrow the style or concept of a picture used in a professional layout. The display type is a different story, though. With the right software and a little trial and error, I can successfully emulate many of the dramatic effects I find in print.

My favorite hunting ground for great display type is glossy magazines — both the editorial spreads and the ads. Certain magazines are especially useful in this regard. I think the folks at *Premiere*, a popular movie magazine, get a tremendous amount of mileage out of their typography. *Rolling Stone* is another good source, and so is *The New York Times Magazine* section.

Note that I rarely look for handbill and flyer ideas in other people's handbills and flyers. One reason: I don't get that many samples in my day-to-day existence, while I'm swamped with magazines of every size and description. More to the point, though, most of the flyers I do see look fairly crummy. It's as if the businesses producing

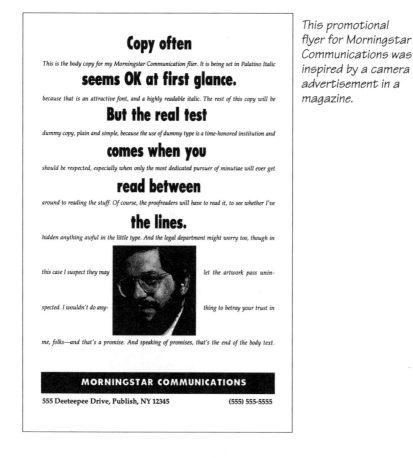

Copy often

This is the body copy for my Morningstar Communication flier. It is being set in Palatino Italic

seems OK at first glance.

because that is an attractive font, and a highly readable italic. The rest of this copy will be

But the real test

dummy copy, plain and simple, because the use of dummy type is a time-honored institution and

comes when you

should be respected, especially when only the most dedicated pursuer of minutiae will ever get

read between

around to reading the stuff. Of course, the proofreaders will have to read it, to see whether I've

the lines.

hidden anything awful in the little type. And the legal department might worry too, though in

this case I suspect they may   let the artwork pass unin-

spected. I wouldn't do any-   thing to betray your trust in

me, folks—and that's a promise. And speaking of promises, that's the end of the body text.

MORNINGSTAR COMMUNICATIONS

555 Deeteepee Drive, Publish, NY 12345   (555) 555-5555

This promotional flyer for Morningstar Communications was inspired by a camera advertisement in a magazine.

these flyers decided that quick, cheap design was a prerequisite to using an inexpensive quick-print shop for reproduction purposes. What a mistake! If you're going to say it at all, say it with class, and there's no reason even simple black ink on white paper can't drip with class if you borrow creatively from the graphic pros.

As a sample exercise, I sat down with a pile of magazines and a concept I've been toying with. My writing business has not been as busy as it might be lately, so it's probably a good time to remind my past and prospective clients that I'm here. In the figure at right, you'll see a version of one possible flyer to serve that purpose, drawn from graphic concepts I found in an ad for Olympus cameras. Incidentally, the concept of interspersing lines of headline text with body text has apparently become something of a trend lately — I've seen very similar designs used by a variety of advertisers lately. As I said, borrowing is the way styles are born.

Learn to Read a Design

The underlying strategy in learning to borrow designs effectively is to start reading everything that comes through your hands on two levels — what the words say, and what graphic means were used to convey and enhance that message. That way, you can identify graphic concepts that may come in handy down the road and stow them away in an idea file, ready to use when the right job comes along.

And of course, copying is a way of learning in its own right. Think of all those art students you see in museums, busily reproducing the works on display to build up their own talents. If you start out as a skillful graphic imitator, you may well begin developing your own innovative and original graphic design concepts.

And then I can start borrowing from you, too.

A Small but Significant Caveat

When my advice on borrowing design elements first appeared in *Home Office Computing* magazine, I received a blistering response from a reader who accused me of the vilest forms of plagiarism, and claimed that following my advice would lead to illegal practices.

I will give an inch to this attack by warning you against copying any design in an attempt to defraud the recipient of your work. That is to say, if I wanted to create a logo for a company in the computer business named American Business Machines and came up with the company initials rendered in light blue stripes, I'd be infringing on the legal rights of IBM.

Company logos are a sticky point, since they are subject to trademark and registration protection. However, publication design is not and cannot be copyrighted. In fact, as the situation now stands, even typeface designs cannot be copyrighted under U.S. law.

If you want to look just like *Time* magazine you're allowed to look just like *Time* magazine as long as you don't try to convince anybody that they're buying *Time* magazine when they're actually buying your publication.

I'm all for originality in design. I urge you to gain inspiration from the publications around you and interpret what you see in ways that appeal to your own aesthetic sensibility. But I'm also a realist, and copying elements of a professionally designed publication is an effective way for the nonprofessional to turn out decent-looking projects on a budget.

ADDING COLOR INEXPENSIVELY

Color on the printed page is powerful.

Our eyes are drawn to color. You can use it in your design to focus reader attention on particular areas of the page.

Color can add excitement to a layout and break up dense sections with contrasting highlights.

It can be used to establish identity — think about Coca-Cola's red and white, Kodak's orange, and IBM's big blue.

Color also provides an opportunity to make your printed material stand out from the crowd. Look at the pile of mail that arrives at your house each day. Aren't you inclined to reach for the flyers and envelopes that catch your eye with color?

For all its virtues, though, working with full color is an expensive proposition. It involves preparing color separations and running on color printing presses. In fact, sometimes that extra expense is part of the message you're trying to communicate. Would you give much credibility to a black-and-white brochure selling a $200 collectible doll? Of course not! You want to see it in a nicely reproduced color photograph.

You can enjoy many of the benefits of color in your publications without investing in full-color printing, though. Using a colored paper stock or colored ink can draw attention to your publication. And adding a single color as a highlight is relatively inexpensive, practical even for small press runs, and as convenient as going to your local print shop.

The Simplest Options

Look at your standard printed output — black ink on white paper. Then consider changing the color of either one, or both. These are inexpensive changes that can make a real impact.

The right choice of an alternate paper color depends on the kind of impact you're trying to make. A flyer announcing the opening of a new card store in my neighborhood was printed on bright yellow paper and caught my eye in a positive way. I would have laughed at a corporate newsletter in the same color scheme.

On the other hand, I received a very elegant newsletter recently that employed both colored paper stock and colored ink to good advantage. The paper was a very light gray, the ink a dark brown — the effect was pure class all the way.

And it didn't cost a fortune to produce either.

A multitude of paper colors are manufactured, but check with your printer to see what he or she has available: Special orders can mean additional expense. And be sure to consider more than just the color of the paper. Texture and weight of paper stock carry their own clear messages to the recipient as well.

Colored inks offer even more variety of choices than paper, but some are considered "standard" while others are "custom." Your printer probably stocks a standard red, a standard green, and so on. If you require a more precise selection, you can order a PMS color.

The Pantone Matching System, or PMS, is the industry's standard system used to specify shades of spot color inks. You can buy a swatchbook with samples of PMS colors at your graphic arts supply store. There are hundreds of subtly different shades from which to choose, each with a unique identification number. Note that colors reproduce differently depending on the type of paper you're printing on — brighter and more vibrant on coated paper, more subdued on uncoated. Be sure you're looking at the swatch printed on the kind of paper you're using when choosing a PMS color.

When selecting colored inks or papers remember that maintaining plenty of contrast is essential. If the paper is too dark or the ink too light, readability will suffer.

An Additional Color

Even a small print shop can produce work with two colors of ink. The paper is put through the press once for the first color, then again for the second. The use of a second-color ink is called a "spot color." It can work well to add highlights to a layout and lead the reader's eye to sections of the page.

There are many ways to use spot color. Company logos and publication nameplates can "pop" off the page. Using large capital letters in a second color will lead the reader's eye to the beginning of each article in a newsletter. Colored line art or graphs add a nice visual texture to a page.

You can use a solid second color, or you can use shades of color by employing screens. Using the same color ink in different percentage screens is a prime technique for making your page look more colorful without adding significantly to the cost of the job.

We'll discuss the details of communicating your color choices to the print shop in Chapter 11.

CHAPTER 8

Newsletters

A really great newsletter could look like hell and still be a really great newsletter.

In fact, that's a great tradition among newsletter publishers. Typewritten copy, inexpensively reproduced on a page with a decent-looking banner identifying the newsletter at the top, and filled with indispensable information. If you're delivering investment advice that's going to make the recipient rich, or up-to-the-minute information in a specialized field that isn't covered elsewhere, then you don't have to worry much about good looks. In fact, that grungy kind of hot-off-the-presses look adds a certain credibility to the down-and-dirty basic newsletter.

Of course, desktop publishing has challenged this traditional approach by making it just as easy to make something reasonably good-looking as something slapdash. Even more to the point, most newsletters today aren't delivering breathlessly awaited insider information — they're information-bearing promotional vehicles. And like any promotional tool, you have to look good to gain a share of the busy reader's time and respect for the publication's contents.

Let's not leave the lesson of old-fashioned newsletter publishing behind too quickly, though. In newsletter publishing, content is king. Even if you're giving the newsletter away free of charge, you are still asking the recipient to invest the time and effort required to read the publication in an era when reading is an unpopular way of ingesting information.

So what makes good newsletter content?

NEWS REPORTING

No, it is *not* trite to say that it's a good thing to put news in a newsletter, because plenty of newsletters contain no real news at all. They contain thinly veiled advertisements. They have announcements of special promotions or sales. They have historical tidbits you might not otherwise have known. They may even have some form of analysis of last month's news events (an accountant's newsletter discussing recent tax rulings, for instance). But none of that is *news*.

News is information that just happened. Odds are, word of the event hasn't reached the recipient yet. It may be the result of privileged information or sources unavailable to others. It is perishable, valuable, attention-getting, and powerful as the "hook" to draw a reader into your newsletter.

To the degree that you have news available to disseminate through your newsletter, you should feature it prominently. Articles that massage egos involved in the newsletter production (Words from the Editor or a nice photo and caption about the boss's spouse's favorite charity fund-raiser) should be diplomatically consigned to a less prominent spot. And the presentation of a news item should reinforce its importance through the use of eye-catching headlines (perhaps with a subhead as well) and illustrations if they're appropriate.

BROWSABLE MATERIAL

Faced with the bulk of bulk-rate print delivered to them on a regular basis, most people have become proficient skimmers. If you can catch their attention as they pass through, you may entice them to continue reading. Even if they only read one tidbit you offer, and that tidbit is enlightening or entertaining enough, you may have made the good impression you were after.

A prime example of the thinking behind this approach is the annual "Dubious Achievements" issue of *Esquire* magazine. It's the only copy of *Esquire* I consistently buy from year to year, because I can have fun with that section. The individual items are rarely more than two paragraphs long. Many are accompanied by photographs, and all have brief boldface headlines that encourage browsing. I'll probably read a few other items in the magazine that month, which I would not have seen without the lure of the Dubious Achievements section. But even if I never get around to reading the short story, the columnists, or the fashion coverage (truth be told, I *know* I won't read the fashion coverage), those entertaining factoids are enough to make me a loyal and satisfied reader.

INFORMATION WORTH KEEPING

Wouldn't it be great if the recipients of your promotional newsletter actually kept it around instead of tossing it in the paper recycling pile? That way, when they needed the service or goods you offer, they'd have your name and number and some information about your company right at their fingertips.

Think about the kind of information that encourages retention. That was a key consideration in a project I undertook for a client. They offer Medicare supplement insurance policies that pay some of the charges the Medicare program omits. It's a highly competitive market, and the company wanted to stand out from the crowd by offering a genuinely useful newsletter to potential customers.

An unusual aspect of this program was the fact that the newsletter recipients were only sixty-four years old — too young to receive Medicare and, hence, too young to order Medicare supplement insurance. Part of the marketing challenge was getting these folks to keep the newsletter on the shelf until they were ready to take action (a few months down the line).

One strategy for accomplishing this goal was to deliver, along with the first issue, a folder for keeping the entire newsletter series.

The second was to incorporate an editorial feature in each issue that would have continuing value to the recipient. For example, we created a quick guide to the Medicare system to serve as an ongoing ready reference source. We included a chart in one issue that let readers determine how long money in an interest-bearing account would last if it were withdrawn at a given rate. In another issue we included a fill-in-the-blanks chart to be used when shopping for

Medicare supplement insurance, to make feature comparison among different policies easier.

Analyze your own newsletter topic and consider areas that lend themselves to encouraging retention.

A travel agency might provide an international currency conversion guide.

A lawn-care business could incorporate a pictorial chart for identifying garden pests.

A computer consultant might prepare a troubleshooting guide for emergency use when the recipient's machine acts up.

ENCOURAGE ACTION

Reading is one way for the newsletter recipient to get involved with your company. But if you can carry the interaction a step further, you move the newsletter up a notch in perceived importance.

The way you accomplish this participatory readership will, of course, depend on the nature of your newsletter. One tried-and-true method is to encourage reader correspondence. Letters to the editor offer a chance to talk back, to climb up on a soapbox, and have the reader's viewpoint expressed. Often this man-in-the-street feedback makes for lively reading in its own right.

Another way to encourage reader interaction is by establishing a feature where their questions are answered.

Still another strategy involves keying additional offers off newsletter materials. How many loyal Ann Landers readers have written in over the years for her brochure about the dangers of heavy petting? Do you have additional information you can provide for interested readers? If they read your offer, write in, anticipate the receipt of additional materials, and finally receive and enjoy them, you have effectively integrated your newsletter and your company into their consciousness over a lengthy period of time.

Other potential involvement devices include special offers and coupons, seminar and meeting invitations, polls and surveys.

NEWSLETTER DESIGN GUIDELINES

In addition to the design concepts presented in Chapter 7, here are some pointers to keep in mind when tackling a newsletter design.

Design a Physical Format First

Before you start worrying about the niceties of column structures, typesetting, and illustration, decide on the broad-stroke issues:

- Will the newsletter be folded or delivered flat?
- How large will the pages be?
- How many pages will there be in each issue?
- Will there be a binding? Staples? Hole-punching for a ring binder?

The answers to these questions will depend on several factors.

Delivery method is an important consideration. If you are going to mail the newsletter, you must decide whether it will be sent in an envelope or include a panel for address and postage. You'll also want to carefully watch the weight of the newsletter and its effect on your postage costs. The choice of mailing method conveys a message of quality to the recipient. An envelope connotes higher perceived value. So does first-class versus bulk rate postage. It's up to you to decide whether the impression conveyed is worth the extra money invested.

The physical format of your newsletter conveys a message too. Oversize pages (bigger than 8½ by 11 inches) attract attention through their unusual size. They indicate that the sender is willing to invest extra money in communicating with the recipient. They are also more work to produce than a page that fits a standard format and cost more to print and to mail.

Don't decide on the shape and size of your newsletter based on your own whim. Consult with the print shop that will reproduce the newsletter to determine what sizes are most economical and practical for the printing presses available. Speak with your local postmaster to evaluate your postage options. And examine samples of other newsletters likely to be reaching your target audience to determine what those folks are used to seeing.

Establish Consistency

A newsletter tries to establish a continuing relationship with its readers. This is conveyed visually by maintaining a consistent look in each issue, with distinctive graphic highlights that make the reader say, "Oh sure, I read this last month" when it arrives.

PILLOW TALK

○ *A Newsletter from Acme Bedding Company* ○

TOYS & GIRLS

Fun and Surprises from Sally's Doll Shop

Sometimes interesting display type is the key to an eye-catching banner. Here we've drawn on two fonts from the Image Club library: Too Much Shadow for the Pillow Talk name, and Jazz Poster for Toys & Girls.

The most prominent distinguishing feature is the presentation of the newsletter title. Often referred to as the *banner* (or sometimes as the *flag*), the name of your newsletter conveys a message about the style and importance of what follows. You can create an elaborate banner if it suits your purposes, perhaps incorporating an illustration or using dramatic display type. However, some of the best banners are the simplest ones, created directly in your page-layout software with well-chosen type and line treatments.

Another area where consistency both from issue to issue and from page to page is important is the column layout of your publication. If you are most comfortable with a simple layout, stick with two or (preferably) three columns of equal width, with headlines that span multiple columns.

If you feel more adventurous, experiment with a grid structure for your newsletter. The grid system is often used by professional designers to combine a solid, basic structure with substantial layout flexibility.

A grid essentially breaks the page up horizontally into a series of equal columns. But this does not mean that each item in your newsletter takes up a single grid column. You might establish a six-column grid, set body type in two-column-wide blocks, and let your headlines span three columns each. You might also vary the use of the grid from page to page. With the same six-column grid, you might use three of the columns for body text in one story, with the other three columns used for illustrations and captions. The body text width is no longer absolutely consistent from page to page, but the underlying grid structure holds the publication together.

Another area where consistency is important is type selection. The key here is to create a hierarchy of type treatments to be used for elements within the newsletter — major story heads, minor story heads, subheads, illustration captions, masthead information, body text, and so on — and stick with those specifications. Unlike a magazine layout, where there is lots of space and the opportunity for large, playful display type headings, a newsletter is more tightly constructed. Readers rely on the visual cues provided by type treatment to rank the newsletter stories in importance. Consistent type treatment offers busy readers a sort of visual outline to your newsletter contents, in addition to being aesthetically pleasing.

Lead the Reader

You know what's in your newsletter — your reader is encountering the material for the first time. As a sensitive editor/designer, it's your job to visually lead the reader through the publication.

This is accomplished partly by placing the most important items in the most prominent position on the page — that is, right at the top, with a highly visible headline to draw the reader's attention.

Illustrations are also sure to draw the reader's eye. However, there is danger in using too many illustrations, each reproduced at a small size. None of them will stand out, and the structure of the page deteriorates into a bland high school yearbook gray mush. Instead, select the illustration that best suits both the sense of the story and the need to interest and amuse your readers and feature it in a prominent size and position. If that means relegating secondary illustrations to a small size or to the trash bin, that's perfectly alright. Better one dramatic highlight than a lot of boring little squibs.

What about stories that continue from page to page? One school of thought advocates avoiding these at all costs. Readers don't like having to jump all over the place to find the end of the article they're reading.

That's a fair point, up to a point. But in addition to the simple truth that story continuations are sometimes editorially inevitable, they also serve a valid function in making your newsletter work by carrying the reader into those inside pages.

If you approach the process strategically, you can get a lot of mileage out of continuations. For example, you would never put a promotional coupon on the first page of your newsletter — it's crass and cheapens the initial impact of the publication. However, there's no reason you can't continue the lead story from page 1 onto page 5 — and lo and behold, at the bottom of the page, right below the story continuation, there's your coupon.

What takes the sting out of continued stories for the reader is to clearly label not only where the continuation is going to appear but where the continued section originated. That is, clearly state "continued on page such-and-such" at the end of the initial story block, then include a shortened version of the story headline and a prominent "continued from page so-and-so" where the remainder of the story appears. You might even reuse an illustration from the story opening, or a small section cut from a larger illustration, in order to provide a visual cue to the reader looking for the end of the story.

And while I am not from the "no continued stories" crowd, I would be loathe to make a reader jump more than once to finish an article.

Leave Some White Space!

There always seem to be more words than there is space to put them all. The natural tendency, then, is to cram as many words as possible on each page, filling up all that wasted blank space with precious information.

Fine. You feel good because you know that you've given your reader all the information you had to dispense. And the reader? What reader? Your prospective reader took one look at that intimidating mass of black type and decided to watch television instead.

Newsletters are rarely light and airy. It is the nature of the form that the information density will be pretty high. However, if you don't give the reader a bit of visual breathing space every so often, all but the most dedicated will find your publication hard slogging indeed.

Leave some white space around your headlines, and some air between columns. Try to incorporate illustrations that are not necessarily full-column rectangles. You can even "hang" columns of text from the top of the page, allowing them to fall short of the bottom margin to produce an interesting rippled lower edge and a little welcome white space.

A STEP-BY-STEP NEWSLETTER PROJECT

For illustration purposes we'll put together the front page of a newsletter called *SquawkTalk* designed to serve the needs of our nation's chicken farmers.

1. Write Your Text With a Word Processor

Create your story text with your favorite word-processing program. Ideally your page-layout program should be able to accept files in the format your word-processing software produces. That way you will maintain text formatting, such as italicization, from the original file. If your word processor and page-layout program are not file-compatible, you can always save the text file in ASCII format. ASCII is a kind of lingua franca in computing: Every page-layout program will accept ASCII text files. However, all formatting beyond the basic text and paragraph breaks is lost.

It's often a good idea to save each headline and each article in a separate file, since they will be printed in different type sizes and styles. Alternatively, I often type the headlines directly onto the page layout using the text-handling capabilities of my desktop publishing program.

2. Create and Gather Illustrations

In this case I combined several pieces of clip art to create two illustrations.

The road in this illustration is a clip-art image included in the *Arts & Letters Editor* package. The chicken comes from the T/Maker EPSF clip-art collection. I brought both images into *Arts & Letters*, adjusted their sizes and the shades of gray used to fill them, and saved them together in a new EPSF file.

Similarly, the line of chicks was composed of multiple copies of a single *Arts & Letters* clip-art image. I edited the graphic to remove the unwanted egg from the picture, duplicated the result, and filled the chicks with varied shades of gray. The chick peeking out of its shell is a separate *Arts & Letters* image. Once again I combined the component parts and saved the resulting image as an EPSF file.

3. Make Rough Layout Sketches on Paper (Thumbnails)

After text is written and graphics are ready, it's time to design a layout — using pencil and paper. In my experience it's wise to resist the temptation to move directly to the computer. You'll get better results if you begin with a set of small thumbnail sketches, then go

By editing, shading and rearranging these clip-art elements, I produced the illustrations needed for SquawkTalk.

on to draw larger version of promising design. You can always adjust sizes and add finishing touches on the computer, but a rough sketch is an important first step.

This is a good time to determine rough type specs for the newsletter. However, leave some mental flexibility so you can evaluate the results as they develop in sample printouts and try new approaches.

4. Transfer Your Rough Layout to the Computer

Finally it's time to load your page-layout software and design the page. The first step with most page-layout programs is to create a set

Build the basic structure of your newsletter by designating column guides and frames with your page-layout program.

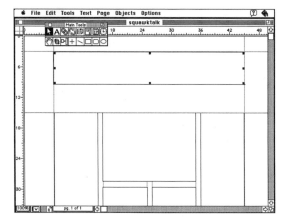

of columns and, within those columns, rectangular boxes to hold your text and graphics (these boxes are often called *frames*).

The column guidelines are placed on-screen using a page setup dialog box that asks for page size, margins, and the number of columns. Frames are then created with your mouse by dragging a box from the top left to the lower right corner of the rectangular frame. You don't have to build the frames perfectly the first time. It is a simple matter to adjust the size and shape until you get it right, even after you've placed your text or graphics inside.

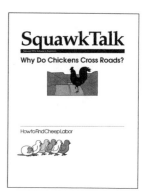

5. Place Text and Graphics on the Page

Place your prepared text and graphic files in the appropriate frames, then assign type specifications to each text section. Crop and size the graphics until they fit well in the space available. Next juggle, adjust, edit, and fine-tune until everything reads and looks right.

Some of this work can be done on-screen, but don't hesitate to print out frequent samples as the page develops (as shown here). It's much easier to proofread text on paper and to get an overview of how the page looks when you have a full-page printout in your hands.

The program breaks the text automatically with hyphens to improve the spacing of justified lines. Sometimes the results are technically correct but don't look right. You can adjust these odd breaks by editing on-screen.

In the sample newsletter I relied on two typeface families built into most PostScript printers. "SquawkTalk" is set in 94-point Palatino Bold. The main headline is set in 32-point Avant Garde Gothic Demi (i.e., moderately bold), with the secondary headline ("How to Find…") in 24-point Avant Garde Gothic Book (i.e., regular). Body text is 11-point Palatino (with 12-point leading), and the table of contents is 10-point Palatino Italic.

After setting up a basic column structure, I like to roughly position my illustrations, then add the text, then fine-tune spacing and add ruling lines. However, there's no "correct" order to follow. Do what works for you.

NEWSLETTER DESIGN IDEAS

A two-column newsletter format is very quick and easy to assemble. You don't want to juggle too many elements on a two-column page, though.

A three-column format offers more flexibility: illustrations can span one, two, or all three columns, there's more opportunity for beginning multiple stories on page 1, and the columns are a comfortable reading width.

There's no rule saying that all of your column widths must be equal. This layout is based on three columns: the left column is half as wide as the other two.

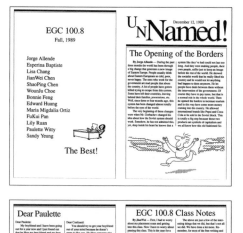

Just because the paper that comes out of your laser printer is an 8 1/2- by 11-inch rectangle doesn't mean your newsletter has to take that shape. My friend and fellow desktop publisher Roni Keane created this small-format newsletter based on her students' writings. Working with the page in landscape orientation (i.e., holding the paper sideways), she laid out two pages on each sheet, printed each page front and back, folded the printouts in the center and stapled them along the spine to create a neat-looking publication with 5 1/2- by 8 1/2-inch pages.

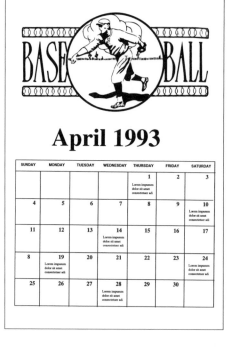

Here's an idea for a large-format single-sheet newsletter that's likely to stay in the recipient's home for a full month after receipt. A large sheet is folded down to create four newsletter pages. When unfolded, the inside reveals a monthly calendar.

CHAPTER 9

Flyers and Brochures

Roughly put, a flyer is a single-page promotional publication while a brochure is a multi-page promo piece. We could slice and dice the categorization more finely. When is a flyer a handbill? If you fold a flyer, does it become a folder? Is a multi-page publication bound by a staple in the upper left a true brochure? How many typefaces can dance on the head of a pin?

What makes this diversity of nomenclature interesting isn't pinning names on each variety, but the diversity of form and function the discussion implies. Printed materials used for business promotion range from a simple one-page announcement of an upcoming sale to catalogs presenting detailed descriptions and illustrations of an entire product line. And with desktop publishing technology, you can explore both basic formats and more complex undertakings from the comfort of your own computer, experimenting with as many alternatives as your imagination can muster until you hit the perfect combination of copy and design.

A QUESTION OF ATTITUDE

There is one overriding principle when creating any promotional literature: View the offer you're making from the prospective customer's perspective.

This can be extraordinarily difficult. After all, what if the X52 Turbo-powered Ultrasonic Laser Button Fastener is your baby. You've nurtured it from a raw idea to a mature product ready for market. Its success or failure will determine whether your oldest kid gets braces or not. And the recipient of your promotional material couldn't care less about any of that.

One tried-and-true formula for shifting your perspective is to focus your presentation on benefits, not on features.

What's the difference?

A feature is that really cool polyethylene molded fastener retainer container that holds 2,000 button-affixing grommets in a tetrahedron configuration to minimize coil deformation.

A benefit is the fact that the product can attach buttons in seconds. Another benefit: It does the job for pennies apiece. Another benefit: There's a complete money-back guarantee.

You see the point. Readers don't want to know about the product per se. They want to know what the product can do for them. Only then, when you've piqued their interest by promising them a valid benefit, can you explain *how* this miracle will occur. And even then, you must keep the level of detail appropriate to the sales job at hand.

KEEP IT SIMPLE

Once you have zeroed in on the information to convey, the next goal is to deliver that information in the most readily accessible way possible. Learning more about your product or service should be a pleasant experience or, at the very least, not a burdensome task.

Putting this advice into practice is a matter of both writing and design. Here are some suggestions to help guide your thinking.

Analyze the Task at Hand

Before you start creating the promotional piece, determine your goal and what it will take to achieve it.

For example, let's say you're producing a flyer to promote a flower shop. Are you trying to build up awareness of the shop's presence? Look for a way to get customers in the door for that crucial first visit. Perhaps you could offer a single free rose to anyone who comes in with your flyer. Or you might want to take a warm and fuzzy holiday-themed approach to encourage people to celebrate an occasion with flowers.

Do you want to increase your business among corporate customers in the area? Stress reliability. Offer to set up a corporate account. You might even preprint a Rolodex card with your name and number and include it with your promotional literature.

The point is, promotional materials without a consciously selected target audience and a strategic marketing goal driving them are rarely successful. Desktop publishing makes it simple to create versions of promotional materials targeted to serve different purposes, and short-run printing capabilities further encourage this strategy.

Organize Your Material

Don't expect your prospective customers to search for the information they need. Once you've determined the facts that must be presented and have a rough idea of the graphics available to illustrate your presentation, organize it in a way that makes the material easily digestible.

The first step is to determine a logical flow. Outline your material, even if it's only a one-page flyer. What is the first item the prospective customer should know? What will reinforce that point? What logically follows from the preceding statement? In this way, you won't fall into the trap of referring to information in paragraph 3 that won't be presented until paragraph 12. Remember, you already know the material, so you're inclined to take a lot of knowledge for granted. Strip the material down to its essentials in outline form and the flaws in the logical flow may appear.

Once you have a progressive presentation outlined, use the words and the design together to lead the reader through your promotional piece. Headings and subheads are an important factor here. They should be comprehensible at a glance, adequate to let the reader know what he or she is likely to find in the body text that follows, and bold enough to catch your eye at a glance.

"At a glance" is an important phrase in this context. Promotional literature is not like a novel, which is consistently read from front to back. Promotional literature is fodder for browsers. A single-page flyer may get only a quick, cursory glance: If there's nothing to catch the reader's attention immediately, you may well have lost your chance to deliver the message.

Even a full-fledged color brochure is often given the "riffle test." The prospective reader holds it in one hand along the binding and riffles through it with the thumb of the other hand. A well-organized design with clearly highlighted headlines and attractive presentation can make enough of an impression in that momentary gloss to invite further attention. Overly packed, gray-looking pages will consign the brochure to the recycling bin.

Write Tight

Assume your reader hates to read. Let's face it, this isn't a new Stephen King novel you're delivering — it's information about a product or service. The fewer words it takes to convey your message, the more likely you are to get those words read.

At the same time, there are times when details are essential to a reasonable understanding of your offer. In those cases, try segregating the nitty-gritty facts from the body of the presentation. A separate box with product description details and statistical information will offer in-depth information to those who want it without disrupting the flow of your larger presentation. And for those who zero in on that kind of information, boxing it (perhaps with a distinctive border) makes it easier to find than burying the stats in the body text.

Let There Be Lightness!

White space is not simply a blank area you forgot to fill. It actually communicates useful information.

A photograph of the X52 Turbo-powered Ultrasonic Laser Button Fastener sitting in a rectangle bordered on all sides by text makes the product look relatively unimportant. But give that same photograph a page or even half-page of its own, bordered by a generous swath of white space, and it suddenly commands attention.

White space is like the setting for a jewel, making you focus your eye on the valuable piece in the center.

Also keep in mind my assumption that your reader hates to read. If that's the case, then white space is a gift. I can read the modest amount of text on the page and then experience the enjoyment of turning another page. Pure pleasure.

Reinforce Your Identity

Don't assume that your reader will remember who you are from the front page to the back page of a flyer or from page 1 to page 3 of a brochure. You want to constantly reinforce your identity in the mind of the recipient.

Take our florist as an example. There are probably four or more competitive flower shops in the same market area. To achieve a disproportionate share of the prospect's mental real estate, our desktop publishing florist needs a memorable name and a distinctive presentation. A striking logo is an excellent tool in this regard. In a multipage brochure that logo should appear on every page (perhaps as an element in a running footer treatment).

Delivering your address repeatedly is important, and a phone number is essential. Customers have been trained to reach for the phone today (and increasingly for the fax machine as well). Don't make your prospects hunt for your phone number. Feature it prominently and repeatedly in your printed piece.

Get Another Opinion

I hate submitting my work for criticism, and I suspect many of you feel the same way. However, the unfortunate truth is, we all have blind spots, fixed opinions, and an awe-inspiring capacity for self-deception.

When it comes to promotional materials, you really should grit your teeth and submit the desktop-published drafts to an "editorial review board" of your own, whether it consists of your spouse, your friends, or better yet, acquaintances who don't mind hurting your feelings.

Of course, invalid criticism is an occupational hazard, and it is entirely possible that you can be right and your critics can be wrong.

However, if you direct your informal review board's attention to particular areas, you can undoubtedly receive valuable input.

For example, ask if they understand the material presented. Do they feel anything is missing? Are there places you've repeated yourself?

Is it clear what you want the reader to do after reading the piece? Is the offer comprehensible and compelling?

Are the graphics attractive? Do they clearly illustrate the product being offered (if appropriate)?

Finally, what impression do they receive about the company presenting the promotional piece?

There is another approach to getting outside guidance on your promotional literature: testing. I'm not talking about locking a group of people in a room with a one-way mirror, a moderator, and a plate of free sandwiches. I mean distributing a promotional piece with a distinct call to action and counting the number of responses it generates.

Desktop publishing is particularly suited to this kind of testing since producing multiple versions of a document is relatively simple. Say you're planning to include a coupon in a flyer.

Is $1 off too little to draw attention?

Would $2 off bring in just as much business as $5 off?

The only way to find out is to create multiple versions of the flyer, with a tracking device built in (a coded coupon, for example), and tallying up the results of a small sample. Then, when you've received feedback from the public, you'll know what offer works best and be ready to "roll it out" to a larger audience.

This approach is standard procedure in the world of professional direct marketing. If you adopt it, here's one more facet of the strategy to try: frequent testing of alternative ideas. The initial piece that has proven its worth is the "control" against which you judge the response to new offers. If your alternative approach proves more successful, it then becomes the control for the next generation of testing, and so on, as you fine-tune your flyer or brochure for maximum profitability.

FLYER AND BROCHURE DESIGN IDEAS

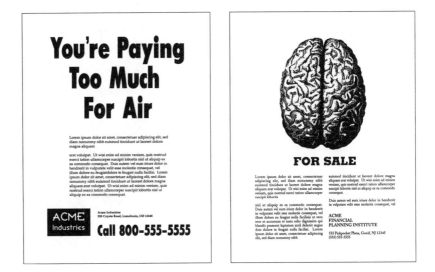

You have to catch someone's attention right away with a flyer. To accomplish this feat, grab them with a bold, compelling headline or an attention-getting illustration.

Here are two more ways to make someone hesitate before passing the bulletin board where your flyer is posted or tossing your handout unceremoniously in the circular file. In the example at left I've used a decorative border (provided with Microsoft Publisher) to make the page distinctive. I created the flyer at right using CorelDRAW and one of the PostScript backgrounds provided with the program.

Design a folded brochure as a strategic whole, rather than as a set of discrete individual pages. In this example (created on an 8 ½ x 11 sheet), the recipient sees an intriguing cover, opens it to read two more panels (the rightmost panel from the inside and the leftmost from the outside) and finally opens the remaining fold to find a two-page-spread illustration.

CHAPTER 10

A Mixed Bag

If it can be printed on paper, it can be desktop-published — and some desktop publishing projects (such as overhead transparencies) transcend the realm of paper altogether. In this chapter we'll take a brief look at a wide range of projects. Given the variety of material covered, I make no claims for encyclopedic coverage of the subtle nuances or diverse possibilities for each genre. Instead, we'll look at some sample materials and consider some tips and techniques to help you in your own explorations and experiments.

REPORTS AND PROPOSALS

• The underlying strategic concept here is to assume that the recipient of your report or proposal is in a tremendous hurry. If that's the case, you must find ways to make the contents as readily accessible as possible.

• Summaries are one tactic that works. Start the report or proposal with an executive summary that says what the document is about and what it will prove. Additional summaries are appropriate at the end of each major section, clearly labeled and graphically set off from the rest of the material so that the time-sensitive browser's eye will be drawn to the summary sections immediately.

• Segregating a basic presentation of the facts from the supporting data is another worthwhile strategy. This divide-and-conquer approach is reinforced through design that clearly differentiates between the two sections.

• Physical presentation also matters a great deal here. Look into high-grade laser papers for the body of the document and heavier cover stock for the front and back, along with binding services available through local quick-print, copy, and stationery shops. If you frequently prepare reports and proposals, there are binding devices on the market for under $100 that will do a neat job right on your desktop.

• Decide on a design format and stick with it throughout the individual report or proposal and for multiple reports or proposals issued over the course of a project. As we've stressed throughout, this does not have to be an elaborate, ornamental orgy of graphics. Restraint works, as long as it is applied consistently and functionally.

REPORT AND PROPOSAL DESIGN IDEAS

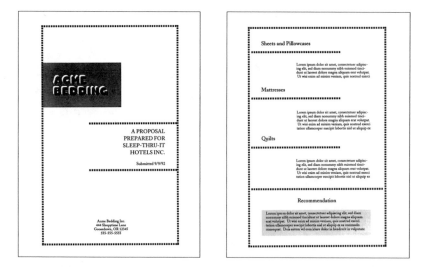

This example strives to achieve two key goals: unifying the presentation through repeated graphic elements (the border and rule treatment) and leading the busy reader to the key decision points (the highlighted Recommendation section).

RESUMES

• Organization is the key to a successful résumé — making the potential employer's job easy by providing quick access to your qualifications.

• Too much ornamentation looks fussy and, worse yet, makes it look as if you've devoted too much time to creating a résumé. You don't want to look like a professional job-hunter, do you?

• Use boldface type for the items that should "pop" when you glance at the page. That includes your name, the categories of material included in the résumé, and (possibly) the job titles you've held.

• Designing a résumé in two columns is often a successful strategy: a narrow column on the left for subheads and a wide column for the body text on the right.

• Ruling lines are often useful in giving a résumé an organized appearance. You may also be able to add a bit of graphic flair through your ruling-line treatment, making the résumé stand out without pouring on the heavy graphic devices.

• Precision counts. Double-check all the spacing between items to be sure you've been consistent. Triple-check the text to be sure it's as tightly worded as possible. And quadruple-check the spelling and punctuation.

RESUME DESIGN IDEAS

Each of these résumé samples uses multiple columns, contrasting typefaces, and ruling lines to bring organization and ease of reading to the page.

BUSINESS FORMS

• The most important individuals in the business-form design and production process are the people who will be using them day in, day out. If that's you, so much the better. But if you're designing forms to be used by others, get them involved in the process. Ask for their ideas at the beginning. Show them each progressive draft as it's completed. Print out a small quantity of samples when you think you're close to the final form and use them for actual on-the-job trial by fire.

• Inevitably the more room you have for writing information by hand, the better. Squeezing in a few extra lines on an order form is clearly counterproductive if it results in squashed, illegible handwriting and inaccurate information.

• As a rule, business forms are not the place for decorative typefaces. Sans serif faces are especially popular in business-form design.

• There are two essential design tools for bringing order to a business form: ruling lines and contrasting weights of type. If you want users of your form to readily perceive the fact that a heavily ruled box is the place to enter the final total, for example, or that the bold-faced words indicate category titles, make the differences between light and bold extreme.

• Remember that your business forms are a significant part of corporate identity. They should carry through on any design themes you have established in the other facets of your business publishing. This certainly includes the use of a consistent company logo and may go further as shown in the examples.

BUSINESS FORM DESIGN IDEAS

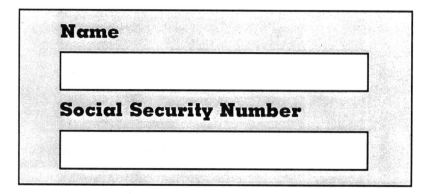

It's sometimes difficult for people to tell exactly where you want them to fill in their information. One strategy to eliminate this confusion is using a light gray tint (10 percent in this case) over the background, leaving the blanks appropriately blank.

This invoice form combines a prominent logo to clearly identify the sender with clearly labeled sections and blank boxes spacious enough to be filled in by hand.

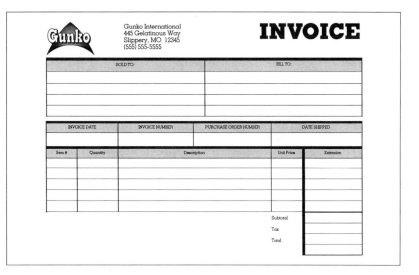

LETTERHEAD AND BUSINESS CARDS

• An elegant, memorable logo is a consummation devoutly to be wished. It doesn't have to be elaborate to be good. In fact, if you think about the really effective corporate logos — the ones that not only look good but instantly make you think of the company name — you'll find simplicity reigns. IBM's horizontally sliced monogram. Apple's rainbow-hued apple. The AT&T "death star."

• The design for your letterhead and business cards should tie together visually. That doesn't mean they have to be identical, but they should use the same typeface and graphic devices (such as logos or ruling-line treatments).

• Business cards are often printed several at a time on a single sheet of card stock and then cut apart by the print shop. For example, if the press prints three cards at a time, this is called running the job "three up." Desktop publishing software makes it simple to duplicate and position your business card design repeatedly on a page to create multiple copies on a sheet. Check with your print shop to determine what kind of mechanical configuration will make best use of their presses.

• If you rarely need business cards, you may be able to get away with printing them directly on your laser printer. Most laser printers will accommodate heavier-weight stock (often by opening a door at the back of the printer to create a straight paper path), although it will still not be as thick as standard business-card stock. Check your laser printer manual for the maximum recommended paper weight and pick up some stock in that weight for experimentation. Avoid heavily textured stock — the laser toner will not stick evenly to the surface. You might also want to spray the printed card with a transparent fixative (available at art supply stores) to keep the laser-printed type from smudging. Again, this is only practical if your needs are limited to a handful of cards each month.

• You may be able to save on preprinted stationery by incorporating your logo and address design as a graphic in the body of your word-processed documents. Many graphically oriented word-processing programs allow you to include graphic images created using illustration software on the printout pages. If your stationery design consists of an all-type treatment, you may be able to re-create it entirely within the word-processing software, including ruling lines and letterspacing modifications where needed.

LETTERHEAD AND BUSINESS CARD DESIGN IDEAS

Your letterhead and business card should be graphically related to reinforce your company identity. This can be accomplished by consistently using a memorable logo, or carrying over a distinctive ruling-line treatment.

OVERHEADS

• The combination of desktop publishing software and a laser printer is a natural for creating overhead transparencies quickly and easily. Just be sure that you buy overhead transparency sheets that are specifically designed for use with laser printers. Laser printers generate high heat in the printing process, and ordinary transparency sheets can melt and jam the printer in truly awful ways. I've had good results with the Laser Transparencies manufactured by Avery.

• The most common mistake in producing overheads is trying to squeeze too much text onto a page. The purpose of an overhead is not to incorporate every word or even every idea in your verbal presentation. The concept behind using overheads with a verbal presentation is to make your key points more memorable by delivering them through two senses, sight and sound. Therefore, the text for your overheads should consist primarily of pithily phrased "hooks" that are likely to stick in the audience's memory.

• Bullets are frequently used to clearly identify the points on the screen where a new idea is presented. To add a little graphic "oomph" to your presentation, explore the many decorative and interesting bullets provided in the Dingbats typeface built into many laser printers.

• Line drawings can be used effectively in an overhead projection presentation. Scanned photographs generally reproduce poorly.

• Use large, generously spaced typefaces for your overheads. If you don't have the opportunity to preview your design by actually projecting the overheads on a screen, try printing them out on paper and holding them at arm's length (or stepping away from your computer monitor and viewing them from across the room).

• If you want to incorporate charts and graphs in your overheads, stick with the basic formats, such as simple bar graphs and pie charts. The complex visualizations of statistics available from today's spreadsheet and charting programs are attractive and often present data effectively, but they're rarely readable from a distance.

• Remember that desktop publishing makes it easy to turn your on-screen presentation into take-away notes for your audience. It's a simple matter to alter the size of the text and illustrations used on-screen, add additional text if needed, and group the resulting material in a convenient format for future reference.

• If you prefer to use 35mm slides for your presentations, look into the powerful presentation software programs on the market today. Products such as *Aldus Persuasion, Micrografx Charisma,* and *Harvard Graphics* are tailored to meet this need, including text handling and graphics creation modules and the facility to output color slides on a film recorder (usually through an outside service bureau).

OVERHEAD DESIGN IDEAS

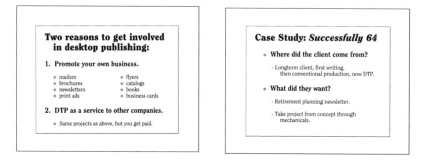

These overheads use a thin ruling-line border to establish a structured appearance. The typeface (Clearface) is decorative but legible from a distance. The scanned sample layouts (below left) and screen shots (below right) worked well as illustrations: The audience was not expected to read the content.

SPACE ADVERTISEMENTS

• Much like a one-page flyer, a space ad to be run in a newspaper or magazine must clearly convey your identity and the information required to contact you. Don't make readers search for this key information. Call their attention to it through careful placement and prominent type treatment.

• If you can come up with a snappy, benefit-oriented headline for a space ad, you're halfway home. Sell the headline with a layout that immediately draws the reader's eye. Leave adequate white space around it, support it with an attractive illustration, use a distinctive (but highly legible) typeface to spark curiosity.

• If you will be advertising repeatedly, try to create a format that will work with minor variations in the illustration and copy over time. This makes producing a series of ads easier, and it also helps establish a visual identity in the minds of the readers. As they browse the pages of a periodical they will spot the "look" of your ad and linger a little longer with it. You may also offer a product or service that is only used occasionally by any individual or business customer. If your ads have a consistent format, the prospective customer can skim the periodical where the ad appears and easily pick out "that Acme ad" from the rest.

• Be sure to check with the publication to determine the exact specifications of the deliverables they require. Most will accept mechanicals, but some require advertisers to deliver films (a company that produces photostats can produce ad films for you). Ad sizes also vary widely from publication to publication — a so-called "quarter-page" ad can be a different size, even in publications that are apparently printed with the same-size pages.

SPACE ADVERTISEMENT DESIGN IDEAS

The distinctive clip art and typography (both from the Image Club collection) in this partial-page ad make the diner look like a fun spot, and graphically reinforces the availability of 24-hour-a-day service.

SAVE BIG AT OUR MAY SALE

Lorem ipsum dolor sit amet, consectetuer adipiscing elit, sed diam nonummy nibh euismod tincidunt ut laoreet

dolore magna aliquam erat volutpat. Ut wisi enim ad minim veniam, quis nostrud exerci tation ullamcorper suscipit lobortis nisl ut aliquip

ex eacommodo consequat. Duis autem vel eum iriure

The Store
4 Grand Ave.
Big Town, USA
12345
555-555-5555

You can make a bold advertising statement without using illustration at all by tapping into the graphic power of dramatic typography.

You don't need elaborate ads to build up recognition over time — just a distinctive graphic element used consistently.

CHAPTER 11

Getting It Printed

I love the smell of printer's ink in the morning. It smells like...
publishing.

Alright, maybe that doesn't have quite the same dramatic impact
as Robert Duvall's battlefield ode to napalm in *Apocalypse Now*, but
the smell of printer's ink really does bring on a distinctive set of
impressions.

It suggests completion of a project: The advance to the commercial print shop to deliver mechanicals indicates that the battle to
meet a deadline is over.

It also suggests tradition. As much as the process of preparing a
publication for the printing press has changed since I edited my high
school newspaper in the sixties, that smell is still the same, and so
are many of the decisions and procedures involved.

The time to get your first whiff of printer's ink isn't once you've
completed the publication, though. If you don't confer with a professional printer early in the process of planning your publication, the
results could be...well, apocalyptic.

THE TAIL THAT WAGS THE DOG

Printing may come at the tail end of your desktop publishing project, but it is very much the tail that wags the dog.

Of course, some projects won't require an outside print shop at all. If you desktop-publish a proposal or report, you'll probably only be making a few copies (albeit a very important few copies), and you can crank those out with your laser printer or a copy machine.

However, as the total number of copies required moves from the tens into the hundreds, it's time to look closely at how you'll have the project reproduced. And the time to do that is as early as possible. In fact, the economics and technicalities of the printing process must be factored in at the initial planning stages. That means before you design a publication, or even commit to undertaking a project. By first understanding the issues involved in getting the ink on the paper, you can determine whether a project is economically viable, and what design decisions can save you time, money, and aggravation down the line.

In this chapter we'll look at two key considerations in getting your project printed:

• Asking the right questions when shopping for printing services; and

• Preparing the materials the right way so that the print shop can reproduce your job.

EXPLAINING WHAT YOU NEED

To plan realistically with a commercial print shop you'll have to provide certain information about your publication and know the right questions to ask. The best approach is not to walk in with hard-and-fast requirements. Sometimes shaving ¼ inch from the printed size, changing your press run quantity, or using a paper or a colored ink that's in stock can save you a significant sum.

Here are the key issues to discuss with your printing professional.

Quantity

When deciding how many copies you will need, remember that a disproportionate share of printing costs represents the steps involved in setting up your publication on the printing press. Once the presses are ready to roll for a 5,000-copy print run, the cost of an extra 1,000 copies will be far less than one-fifth of the original figure. By the same token, if you try to go back for an additional 1,000 copies after the job has run, expect to pay the full cost of making the presses ready to run your job again.

Page Size and Page Count

Your goal here is to use the paper you buy and your printer's press capabilities with maximum efficiency. While you should start out with a general idea of the final size you want, be open to suggestions. Ask the printer for page sizes that will minimize wasted paper.

Not long ago I prepared mechanicals for a magazine based on size specifications provided by the client. With mechanicals ready to ship out I discovered that he hadn't conferred with the printer before determining these specs. To print the job according to those original specifications would have required a nonstandard, larger sheet of paper that would then have to be trimmed down, meaning lots of wasted paper stock. If we shaved the specs by ¼ inch on one side and ⅛ inch on the other, the paper costs would go down significantly. I made the changes to the mechanicals, grumbling all the way. Don't fall into the same trap: determine final page sizes after talking with your printer.

By the same token, there are efficient and inefficient page counts. When designing a booklet or newsletter, multiples of eight-page units are usually the most cost-effective formats for both printing and binding. Adding four pages isn't too bad, but adding six pages is very inefficient (you're usually better off printing an extra eight-page section and leaving the last two pages blank). As you move into book-length publications and larger runs on high-speed presses, planning in 16- and even 32-page units is the most economical strategy. Discuss your options and their cost impact with your printer.

Paper

The kind of paper you use conveys a message just as surely as the words and pictures you print on it. There is a mind-boggling variety of printing papers available, and far too little space here to go into details. Ultimately the best procedure is to determine the effect you are trying to achieve — somewhere on the quick-dirty-and-cheap to rich-and-opulent continuum — and ask the printer to show you some samples.

Of course you'll be interested in cost and appearance when evaluating paper samples, but several less obvious characteristics also come into play.

For example, you know the way ink printed on one side of a sheet of paper sometimes shows through on the other side? The degree of show-through is referred to as the paper's *opacity*. Generally paper with higher opacity is thicker and more expensive. Try to look at a printed sample of the paper you're considering to determine whether its opacity will be adequate for your needs. If you can't find a printed sheet, place a blank sheet over a printed page and judge the show-through that way.

The weight of a paper may not be readily apparent if you're handling single sheets, so try to examine a sample with about the same number of pages you'll be printing.

Keep mailing requirements in mind too. If you're going to be sending your publication, check the costs of different mailing weights in different postal classes. You may want to choose a lighter-weight paper to fit into a more economical category.

If you expect people to write on the printed page, try it yourself with a sample. I still remember with horror a product order form included in a magazine I used to edit. It stubbornly resisted all attempts to write on it with pencils or ballpoint pens, and even a felt-tipped marker smeared if you didn't let it dry completely. A major, major headache.

Finally, ask the printer if the weight and finish of the paper is appropriate for the kind of text and illustrations you'll be printing. This is especially important if you are planning to use photographs or fine-line drawings in your publication.

Colors

The number of colors used in your type and illustrations are a major component in the cost of a printing job.

Full-color photographs and illustrations require *four-color printing* — the images are reproduced by combining different levels of four primary printing colors (yellow, magenta, cyan, and black). This is a demanding, specialized form of printing, and many smaller shops don't handle it. If you require four-color printing, the first question you should ask of a prospective printer is whether or not they offer this capability.

In discussing design in Chapter 7, I mentioned a more economical way to add color to your publication: using colored inks to highlight design elements. The cost of adding a single so-called "spot" color or several additional colors will depend on the type of press to be used in printing the job.

Also consider using a colorless "color" — varnish. In printing, varnish is considered another kind of ink, and priced accordingly. You can use a glossy varnish to add shine to your printed piece or stick with a dull varnish if your goal is simply making the publication more durable. Varnish can even be used as a design element. When my company created a folder for one client, we used glossy stock for the folder and overprinted it with dull varnish that covered most of the surface but left a large, glossy rendition of the company logo showing through. The effect was subtle and very elegant.

Photos and Illustrations

Photographs and illustrations with areas of solid gray or color require several steps for the printer. (Illustrations composed only of black lines and pasted down on your mechanical can be shot with the type and do not cost extra.)

Each black-and-white photograph must be shot separately with a special camera to create a reproduction film (called a *halftone*). For each color photograph the printer must create a *color separation* — four separate films to allow four-color-process reproduction. In either case the films must then be *stripped in* to position with a separate film containing all the type elements of your publication. You will pay for each photograph based on its size and also pay for the stripping process.

Design Elements

Certain design features can create printing problems if you don't discuss them up front with your printer.

For example, you may want to run a photograph right up to the edge of a page. This is called a *bleed* and can be a very effective graphic device. However, as a piece of paper passes through the press it is carried along by a *gripper* along the edge. If you don't place your bleed photographs in acceptable locations, they may interfere with the gripper. Your printer can prepare a diagram showing where a bleed image can and cannot fall.

Similarly, you may want a design element to *cross the gutter* and span two consecutive (facing) pages. Precisely aligning pages to make this work properly can be very tricky, and should definitely be discussed with your printer. If you must cross the gutter, look for ways to position the artwork on the center spread of a printed section. Your printer can tell you where these spreads will fall.

Another design consideration is the placement of color. Depending on the configuration of pages on the press, you may be able to save money by printing only certain sections of your publication in color, yet still have color pages interspersed throughout. Once again, ask the printer.

Folding and Binding

The closer you conform to the printer's standard procedures in these areas, the more economical your job will be. For instance, some high-volume printing presses will fold the paper automatically as it comes off the press, as long as you are using a standard fold. At the other extreme, pages can be folded by hand if necessary, with appropriately high costs.

The binding technique to be used will also affect your design and mechanical preparation. For example, some bindings require that you leave extra room in the gutter.

Delivery and Schedule

Do you want the printer to bundle your printed pieces into pre-counted groups? Do you need pages collated? Do you want the finished job shipped to you or will you pick it up? All of these will affect the printer's estimate.

The tightness of your deadline requirements can also have a substantial impact. Printers like to schedule their work flow to make the best use of their presses. If they can run two or more jobs in a row with the same-size paper, it saves them time and effort. Similarly, it takes time to wash out the presses and add a nonstandard ink color — time that is saved if two consecutive jobs use the same-color ink. If you have the luxury of flexible delivery requirements, you may be able to save some money by letting the printer run your job when it fits easily in the press schedule.

Prints Charming?

Large publishing houses, advertising agencies, and other companies that purchase a lot of printing have in-house production specialists who immerse themselves in the complexities of the printing business and make decisions accordingly. You and I don't have that luxury. Our printing specialist is the printer, and one of the most important factors in getting satisfactory printing work is developing a relationship of trust and cooperation with that vital resource.

For your own peace of mind, that means getting bids from several potential printers on a given project. Bear in mind that each printing company has its own specialty or specialties and its own equipment. The company that offers the best price on an eight-page black-and-white newsletter may be the most expensive choice for a thirty-two-page full-color brochure.

Once you have chosen a printer, though, try to develop a friendly, ongoing relationship. Ask as many questions as necessary, but keep in mind that the printer's time is his or her most valuable resource. Keep last-minute changes to a minimum — those changes are expensive and tend to make you an unpopular client.

And above all, pay your printer's bill on time. A small company that pays its bills within the month can receive a disproportionate share of attention and service when compared to a big company that makes the poor printer wait ninety days for payment!

CREATING MECHANICALS

The term "desktop publishing" is misleading. You're not really publishing with your desktop computer — you're preparing pages (called *mechanicals*) for reproduction.

Even with computer output of "finished" pages, preparing

mechanicals usually requires a little manual labor. And often some rubber cement.

What's a Mechanical?

Mechanicals are a publication's final pages ready for professional printing. Now what does that entail?
  • All of the type is in its precise, final position.
  • Depending on the kind of illustrations, the actual finished artwork may be pasted in place, or positioning indicators on the mechanicals may show where the art is supposed to go.

Mechanicals are called *camera ready* because the printer photographs them with a special camera to produce films, which are then turned into plates for the printing press.

Creating camera-ready mechanicals without a computer requires meticulous hand labor performed by people called *mechanical artists* or, more commonly, *pasteup artists*. Sometimes the job is a breeze — preparing single-column mechanicals for a novel, for instance. But the average magazine page has several columns of type plus illustrations, captions, and page numbers. Thin rules, or lines, and other graphic details may also appear. Using traditional techniques, each of these elements would arrive on separate pieces of paper, and the pasteup artist would have to precisely position them all.

Today we can handle much of that assembly process with the computer. In fact, you can sometimes hand the pages that come from your laser printer or the typesetter's equipment directly to the printing company (a practice found primarily in book publishing).

Most of the time, though, you need to mount the flimsy printouts on stiff boards so that they survive the handling they will receive.

You may need to add illustrations or positioning indicators.

It's often easier to make simple corrections by hand on the boards instead of rerunning an entire page (and it's much less expensive if you're sending the job out for typesetting).

And sometimes limitations in your page-layout software require you to place type by hand. For instance, if your page-layout software won't place type on a diagonal, you may have to manually place a strip of type at the angle you want.

Bottom line, the print shop doesn't care whether you're working with a computer system or a roomful of calligraphically trained chimpanzees — they want complete, traditional mechanicals, just the way they've been getting them for decades. And that requires a little effort on your part.

There may be times when a job is complex and you need a professional pasteup artist. If you don't know one, your printer undoubtedly will have a recommendation, and may have someone on staff to handle the assignment. However, with the computer handling most of the manual-dexterity end of mechanical preparation, even a klutz like me can usually prepare an acceptable mechanical for printing.

The Quality of Your Raw Materials

Type output on a 300-dpi desktop laser printer looks great, right?

Sure it does — until you hold it up next to a professionally printed page of text. Suddenly that laser printer output that looked so crisp and beautiful a moment ago loses some of its appeal.

Laser printing invariably suffers from assorted defects — most notably the "laser stubble" of bumps along curves, the stairstep progression of diagonal lines, and the inability to render really fine lines, like those found in typefaces with hairline serifs. Make no mistake about it, 300-dpi laser printer output is very good. For many projects it's more than good enough. But there are higher-quality alternatives out there that you should know about. Because it doesn't have to cost you an arm and a leg to create output just as sharply detailed and smoothly curved as the pages of your favorite national magazine.

Taking One Step Up

300-dpi resolution is still the standard for laser printers, but it is no longer the only way to go.

Enhanced desktop lasers now offer noticeably better output, as discussed in Chapter 2. Of course, you may not own one of these machines, but that doesn't mean you can't get access to one. Check with your local quick-print shop or copy shop. Many of these operations are installing enhanced laser-printing devices and will accept your files for output at a modest fee (perhaps $1 a page).

When deciding on an enhanced laser output device, keep in mind that the figures you'll see for "resolution" supplied by equipment manufacturers are, shall we say, less than reliable. Often manufacturers will tout the "apparent" resolution, which is not the same as the actual number of dots of toner per inch of paper. The best way to judge is to look at sample printouts. And don't just accept a manufacturer's sample. Have a few pages of your own publication printed out and eyeball the results closely.

Well? Is that type sharp enough yet? Because we have another quality step available to us — imagesetter output. So straighten those bow ties, get your formal gown out of mothballs, and slap another coat of polish on your best pair of shoes. Our desktop publishing projects are going formal!

LOOKING SHARP WITH IMAGESETTER OUTPUT

Hmm...can't seem to find my cummerbund anywhere.

On second thought, let's agree to looking as slouchy as we like, and concentrate on making our publications look as sharp as we can.

That means using an imagesetter, the same equipment used to produce the smoothly curved, crisp-edged type you see in commercial magazines and books. Imagesetters use photographic film and light-sensitive paper to produce their finely detailed output. And they're definitely not the kind of equipment you'd buy for your own office. In addition to being prohibitively expensive, they're maintenance-intensive, technically complex, and demanding to operate.

Luckily you don't have to own an imagesetter to get imagesetter output. There are hundreds of service bureaus across the country that will output your files on their equipment at reasonable prices. And the most exciting part of making the leap from laser printer to imagesetter is that it really doesn't take much to accomplish.

Not much time — the same publication files you create for laser printing can usually be output on an imagesetter, and the extra step won't add more than a day to your production schedule.

And not much money — figure imagesetter output for a 4-page newsletter will cost less than $50 including overnight delivery.

Service Bureaus at Your Service

You say you haven't passed a storefront with a sign saying "Joe's Friendly Service Bureau" on your trips to the market? Can't say I'm surprised. Imagesetter service bureaus are usually located in major metropolitan areas, where the number of professional publishers and advertising agencies in the vicinity will provide a profitable client base. If you're fortunate enough to have a service bureau operating locally, so much the better. There is a certain undeniable comfort in being able to speak face-to-face with the professionals whose services you employ.

But, in this case, geography is not destiny. Whether you live in the heart of Metropolis or 40 miles from your nearest neighbor, quick-turnaround imagesetter output is available to you. Through the miracle of overnight delivery services, you can put your file on a disk and have it reach a distant service bureau the next morning.

Even better, if you own a modem, you can deliver files to the service bureau over the phone and cut both overnight delivery expenses and a day off your schedule.

In fact, I've never set foot in the service bureau I use most often. Like many others, they maintain a bulletin board system that lets me transmit publication files to them via modem. They output these files on Linotronic equipment and return the camera-ready proofs via Federal Express. Even if I upload my files late in the day, I'll have the output on my desk by 10:30 the following morning.

Several manufacturers produce imagesetter equipment, including Compugraphic and Varityper, but the name you'll encounter most often is Linotronic, whose various models currently hold the lion's share of this market.

The high-resolution output business has essentially standardized on PostScript fonts and file formats. With the development of scalable fonts for the Hewlett-Packard Series III, Compugraphic has created the drivers necessary to output HPCL 5 fonts on its imagesetters, but the number of service bureaus supporting this format is relatively small. I'm sure some service bureaus will also be able to handle TrueType fonts, though I don't see TrueType building up much of a head of steam among graphic arts professionals. The most "no-sweat" choice is indisputably PostScript.

CHOOSING A SERVICE BUREAU

If geography is not destiny in this case, how do you find a service bureau?

Check the Ads

Service bureaus usually advertise in the business section and/or the science section. If you don't find what you want in your local paper, go to the library and check out-of-town papers, particularly those from major cities. Some service bureaus cultivating a national clientele also advertise in desktop publishing magazines.

Even if a service bureau is Macintosh-based, it can usually handle PostScript files created with an IBM-compatible PC.

Get Recommendations From Your Local Computer Store

See if they have someone on staff who specializes in desktop publishing.

Go On-Line

CompuServe, America Online, and Prodigy all have active desktop publishing discussion areas. CompuServe is a particularly rich resource, with a general-purpose desktop publishing forum (Go DTPFORUM) and individual forums supporting several DTP vendors' products, including Adobe, Aldus, Hewlett-Packard, and Ventura. Assuming you have a modem installed and an account established, getting advice is easy. Just leave a message describing your needs on an appropriate forum and wait for recommendations.

Get Recommendations From a Local User's Group

Nothing beats firsthand recommendations from local folks who've already tested the waters.

WORKING WITH A SERVICE BUREAU

Microsoft Windows on PC-compatible computers and System 7 on the Macintosh have made it much easier to create PostScript output files for delivery to a service bureau, but there are still plenty of ways to foul up the process of moving your publication from your PC to the service bureau for output. With a little planning, though, you can effectively sidestep them. I'll point out some of the questions you'll have to answer to avoid common pitfalls in a moment. There are two additional resources you'll want to consult, though.

The first is the manual for your page-layout software. The procedures for creating files for imagesetter output vary from program to program. If you have trouble understanding the manual, try calling the software publisher's technical support group or leaving a question on one of the on-line forums.

The second essential resource is the service bureau staff. In fact, since most service bureaus have the technological capability needed to produce perfectly acceptable output, the availability of knowledgeable experts may well guide your selection. PC-based desktop publishers can find themselves on the short end of the stick in this regard, since so many service bureaus are Mac-oriented. Ask questions to ensure that any service bureau you are considering is at least familiar with the PC page-layout software you will be using. Ideally, the service bureau should be running some PCs on the premises, even if they emphasize the Mac side.

Here are some questions you'll have to answer in preparing your publications for the service bureau.

What Fonts Are You Using?

The service bureau must have the same fonts loaded on their system for their output to match your laser-printed proofs. In this case, close is not good enough, and the same font name does not mean you'll get identical output. Typefaces like Times, Helvetica, Garamond, and Century are available from many type houses in many subtle variations. The key problem with substituting between them is the way character widths differ. Even minute differences, when multiplied across all the characters in a block of text, can change the way lines and paragraphs break, which in turn can throw off the entire page layout.

What Resolution Do You Want?

Linotronic imagesetters basically offer two high-resolution choices: 1,270 dpi and 2,540 dpi, with a premium price for output at the higher setting. For text and most computer graphic work there is no reason to pay extra for 2,540 dpi output — 1,270 is more than adequate. The higher setting is better suited for grayscale and color image reproduction.

Does Your Publication Include Graphics?

As a general rule, you'll want to avoid including bit-mapped graphic images (those created with paint programs or scanners) in your imagesetter output. They print much more slowly than type, and service bureaus charge substantial per-hour fees for jobs that take a long time to print. You'll get better print quality and pay less by letting your commercial printer reproduce photos or paint-type images using traditional halftoning techniques.

On the other hand, line drawings created using object-oriented illustration programs (such as *Adobe Illustrator*, *CorelDRAW*, and *Micrografx Designer*) print reasonably quickly and gain dramatically in image quality compared to laser-printer output because they can take advantage of the full resolution of an imagesetter. Watch out for shaded areas, however, and complicated gradated fills in particular, since these can be time-consuming to output.

Do You Want Paper or Film Output?

In order to reproduce your publication, a commercial print shop will eventually have to create films for printing. These films can be output directly from an imagesetter, saving a step — but in most cases I don't recommend it. You can't make manual changes to a publication once it's been output to film. In addition, film must adhere to demanding technical specifications appropriate to the press the job will print on. Rather than become the middleman between the imagesetter and the printer, I prefer leaving the film-making to the print shop.

What Kind of Files Will You Deliver?

This choice will largely be dictated by the service bureau's preferences. Some bureaus prefer receiving files they can load into page-layout software for printing. The advantage here is that they can see what your publication will look like on their own computer screens, identify problems if they exist, and make adjustments if necessary.

Often, though, it is neater and more reliable to deliver PostScript output files. This means that instead of printing your publication directly to a printer, you print it to a file. That file can then be copied to a PostScript output device without having to go through the program used to create the file in the first place.

There are several advantages to delivering PostScript files. It isn't necessary for the service bureau to own the same layout program you are using (often a problem in outputting PC-created files at a Mac-based service bureau). Also, since the PostScript file you create is complete and ready to print, you avoid variations that can be introduced when loading a publication file into someone else's computer setup. If the settings for hyphenation or kerning are different, for example, you can throw off the entire layout.

If you do go the PostScript file route and own a PostScript printer, I find it useful to check that the file was created accurately by copying it to the PostScript printer before sending it to the service bureau. Macintosh users will need a utility program to handle this (widely available from on-line bulletin boards and user groups). PC users can use the DOS COPY command to send the PostScript file directly to the printer. For example, if the file name is YOURFILE.PRN and your printer is connected to LPT1, you would issue the following command at the DOS prompt:

COPY YOURFILE.PRN LPT1: /B

The "/B" parameter lets DOS know you're sending a binary file and is required.

How Will You Deliver Your Files?

You can hand over disks to a service bureau or send files via modem. See if the service bureau can handle compressed files created using utility programs in StuffIt (Macintosh), ARC, or ZIP formats (PC). You can squeeze the file length down, often 50 percent or more, using these utilities, saving substantially in disk space and/or on-line connect time.

Is It Worth the Effort?

There are certain details you simply have to get straight when using an outside service bureau. I'd say it's a fairly steep learning curve, since it all has to be right or the job simply won't come out in a usable form. However, while it may be a steep uphill climb, it's a short one, and once you've got the procedure down pat it becomes virtually automatic.

PREPARING YOUR MECHANICALS

Whether you're using straight-from-the-laser pages or imagesetter output, you'll have to put it all together in the form of camera-ready mechanicals. That means shopping for some tools and supplies, which should be available at virtually every art supply store.

Boards

Mechanicals are often referred to as boards because the type and illustrations are mounted on stiff boards. The actual board you use can vary. If you're preparing only a few pages, use a moderate-weight illustration board. For larger jobs, it's more convenient to use a lighter grade of two-ply Bristol board. Look at an existing mechanical, then take a trip to an art supply or stationery store and check out a few samples.

Rubber Cement and Friends

One popular way to stick paper to board is with rubber cement. It comes in two basic types: two-coat and one-coat. When using two-coat rubber cement, you put a thin layer on both the board and the back of the paper to be glued down, wait for them both to dry, then paste the item down. One-coat is more difficult to find for some reason, but more convenient. You apply one-coat only to the paper, wait for it to dry, and then place it on the board.

Unless you're using very small quantities, you'll want to buy rubber cement by the quart or the gallon and pour it into a special bottle with a built-in brush.

When it comes to preparing mechanicals, rubber-cement thinner is the elixir of the gods. If you need to move a piece of type after it's been pasted down, applying some thinner will loosen it from the board and allow you to make adjustments. Pasteup artists use containers that look like old-fashioned oil cans to apply thinner.

A small roller with a plastic wheel — called a *burnisher* — is another essential tool. It's useful for smoothing the paper down on the board and ensuring even contact.

The last item you'll use when working with rubber cement is a pickup. Inevitably some rubber cement will extend beyond the edge of the paper or drip in an unwanted spot. A pickup is basically a rubber-cement eraser — a rectangular block that picks up rubber cement from the page with a brisk rub.

A very important note about rubber cement and thinner: You must use them in a well-ventilated area, because the fumes can be harmful. For this reason, some pasteup artists use wax instead of rubber cement. However, a tabletop wax machine is an expensive piece of equipment, and the more affordable portable waxers are clumsy at best. Rubber cement is fine, as long as you let some air into the room.

Spray Mount

Nowadays, instead of rubber cement, many pasteup artists prefer a spray-mount adhesive (Scotch is one popular brand). Although more expensive than rubber cement, spray adhesive is easier to work with. It comes in an aerosol can, and you can easily remove any paper pasted down with it without using thinner.

Non-Repro Blue Pens and Pencils

As I mentioned earlier, printing is a photographic process. Sometimes you'll want the marks you make on the mechanical to show, and sometimes you won't. Any old red pen or pencil is fine for marks you want the camera to pick up (such as a quick addition to a rule). However, you'll want a non-repro blue pen or pencil for marks you'd like to disappear when the camera shoots your mechanical.

Table and T Square

If you're serious about mechanical preparation, you'll need a drafting table and a T square. The drafting table has a rectangular working surface and smooth outer edges. The T square has a head and a straightedge mounted at a perfect 90-degree angle. If you hold the head of the T square firmly against the side of a drafting table, the straightedge forms a reliable horizontal, which can be used to align illustrations and other elements on your mechanical.

To make occasional mechanicals using output from your computer, you can get by with a ruler. I would make at least one more addition to your arsenal, though: a plastic triangle. It's relatively easy to draw a rectangular box, or line up items along a perpendicular, if you align one edge of the triangle with a predefined straight line (like the edge of the board) and use the triangle's other edge as your guide.

A Few Odds and Ends

To finish your shopping spree (no complaints, now — most items on the list were pretty inexpensive), you'll need wide masking tape and a pad of tracing paper. The tracing paper should be large enough to cover the entire page area of your mechanical.

You'll want to tape a sheet of tracing paper to the top of each board so that you can lift the tracing paper to read the mechanical. The tracing-paper overlay is usually called a *tissue* and serves a dual purpose. It protects the surface of the mechanical and, since you can still see the mechanical through the tracing-paper overlay, it's also a perfect place to mark information for the printer such as instructions for using color.

Put all this stuff on your worktable at home and your friends will think you really know what you're doing.

COMMUNICATING THROUGH YOUR MECHANICAL

If your project is all text, preparing a mechanical can be as simple as taking the output from the laser printer or high-resolution imagesetter and mounting it page by page. But what if you want to include illustrations in your project? Or add a gray tinted block, or a little color? Read on.

A mechanical is more than a bunch of boards to keep the page elements in place and unwrinkled — it's a means of communicating with the print shop.

What do you need to say, beyond, "Here it is!"?

How about identifying the colors you want in the printed piece, and the size, position, and cropping of the illustrations?

To convey this information we have two ways to send messages to the print shop:

• A sheet of tracing paper is taped onto the top edge of each mechanical board to form an overlay, and special instructions are written on this overlay.

• Simple line-art illustrations should be placed directly on the mechanical. But for highly detailed line art, artwork that incorporates colored areas or photographs, we'll include placeholders on the mechanical and deliver the original artwork to the printer separately with the job.

That's the Size of It

When the size of your original illustration, be it line art or photograph, is not same as the reproduction size you want, you'll need an accurate way to calculate the required reduction or enlargement.

If you're using a scanner, you may be able to size the illustration directly on screen by dragging it with a mouse until it fits the available space on your layout. Even with a scanner, you will have to provide an outside print shop with a percentage of reduction or enlargement for any photograph or illustration that they are shooting for halftone reproduction.

The gadget traditionally used to accomplish this chore is a proportion wheel. Available at any graphic-arts supply store, a proportion wheel consists of two plastic disks, one larger than the other, riveted together in the center to let them rotate freely. Around the circumference of each disk are measurements, and there's a window in the middle. To use the proportion wheel, you align the dimensions of your original photo or artwork on one wheel with the dimensions of the image as it will be reproduced on the other wheel.

Once you have the proportion wheel aligned properly, you can make sure that your image fits in the space allotted to it on the page layout. Let's say I have a photograph that's 10 inches wide and 8 inches high. I want to reduce the width to fit a 4-inch-wide column. According to my proportion wheel, reducing the 10-inch width to fit into 4 inches shrinks the 8-inch original height down to 3³⁄₁₆ inches. If that doesn't correspond well with the space available in my layout, I can either crop the photo or adjust the layout.

The window in the proportion wheel provides a vital statistic: the percentage of enlargement or reduction required to fit your illustration to the layout. In the example above, the photo must be reduced by 40 percent to fit the available space.

If you insist on working with measurements in inches, the proportion wheel is your best bet. But I must confess I had to dig around in my bottom drawer to find my proportion wheel before writing the section above, having long since abandoned it in favor of a pocket calculator.

Since our traditional English measurement system breaks inches into fractional parts, calculating sizes in inches with a decimal-based calculator is more trouble than it's worth. If you're willing to work with the metric system, though, sizing illustrations is much faster, more efficient, and more accurate with a calculator than with a proportion wheel. There are 25.4 millimeters in an inch, so working with millimeters provides highly accurate measurements without resorting to fractions or decimals. And it doesn't matter whether your outside suppliers are using metric measurements or not, since what we're after is a percentage of enlargement or reduction.

Let's size a photo similar to our previous illustration. It measures 250 millimeters (mm) wide and 200 millimeters high. Our column width is 100 millimeters. To figure out how tall our image will be when the width is reduced to fit we use a simple ratio: Divide the original height by the original width to get the proportion, then multiply the result by the reduced width to get the reduced height. In this example, 200 mm/250 mm = .8, and .8 x 100 mm = 80 mm. I find that much easier than working with quarters, eighths, sixteenths, and, heaven forbid, thirty-seconds of an inch.

Now let's find the percentage of reduction by dividing the width of the reduced image by the width of the original: 100 mm/250 mm = 40 percent.

I realize all this multiplication and division may sound complicated as I explain it on paper, but follow along with a calculator and you'll see how fast and natural the process really is.

Now What?

Now you've determined the percentage of enlargement or reduction for your image. What do you do with that information?

If you're working with line art, you have a photostat (stat for short) made of the original. Your printer may have a stat camera, or can certainly tell you where you can have a stat made. A photostat is a clean, crisp photographic reproduction shot to the percentage size you request. You can place the stat in position on your mechanical with rubber cement, spray mount, or wax, and it will be shot along with the type at no extra charge.

If you are working with photographs or fine-line artwork, the best route to high-quality reproduction is to send the original along with your mechanicals and have the printer shoot it to size. The printer produces a photographic negative of your image that is then incorporated with the negative film of the type portion of your page. This is known as *stripping in* an illustration.

You will have to indicate the position and cropping of the illustrations you want stripped in to your page. The best way is to position a photocopy or photostat, reduced or enlarged to size, directly on your mechanical. Be sure to write FOR POSITION ONLY (or shorthand it "FPO") on the photostat or photocopy, to make sure no one mistakes it for final artwork.

It's a good idea to create a line box indicating the correct size and position of the illustration using your desktop publishing software and print it with the text. This box is called a *keyline*. Place the FPO image within that box. If you want the box reproduced on the page as well, be sure to leave about ¼ inch between the FPO copy and the lines of the box.

The final step is marking the illustration and mechanical for reproduction. Attach a strip of paper to the back of each illustration, leaving a border visible from the front. Indicate the percentage of enlargement or reduction, the page on which it falls, and your name and phone number (illustrations from different jobs have been known to commingle at the print shop). To make life easier for the printer, give each illustration a unique number or letter as well, and write this identification on the illustration label and the mechanical overlay. If you want the keyline reproduced, trace it on the overlay and write "Print Keyline."

TINTS, SCREENS, AND SPOT COLOR

Most desktop publishing software allows you to print type in shades of gray or create gray boxes or other shapes, usually in 10-percent increments. This is very useful if your final output will be laser printed, and provides a good indication of tinted areas when printing laser proofs. For final mechanicals, though, you will get superior quality at minimal expense if you have the printer produce the gray shades you want using screens.

The printer's screens are composed of much finer dots than those you can produce with your computer output. This superior resolution is especially important if you are planning to print shaded type or to run type over a shaded box — the edges of the type will be much crisper and more attractive. Even if all you want is a shaded geometric shape, the effect will reproduce more smoothly using the printer's screens.

Indicate the screen you want by using the same 10-percent increments you use within your desktop publishing software. For your mechanical, though, output the type you want reproduced in a tint in solid black. Then, on the overlay, circle the sections you want shaded and write in the percentage of shading you want.

If you want a shaded box, use a keyline on the mechanical and write your instructions on the overlay. As before, if you want the lines of the box to print as well, indicate "Print Keyline."

Colorful Possibilities

How about adding a little color to your publication?

There are two kinds of color printing: process color and spot color. Process color is used for full-color reproduction of photographs and artwork. When it comes to preparing mechanicals, working with full-color illustrations is no different from the steps outlined above for working with black-and-white photographs.

Spot color, on the other hand, is a single color used to highlight elements in your design. Using spot color is much less expensive than full-process color printing, but it can still work well to add interest to a layout and lead the reader's eye to sections of the page.

The Pantone Matching System, or PMS, is the industry-standard system used to specify shades of spot color inks. You can buy a swatchbook with samples of PMS colors at your graphic-arts supply store. There are hundreds of subtly different shades from which to choose, each with a unique number. Note that colors reproduce differently depending on the type of paper you're printing on —

brighter and more vibrant on coated paper, more subdued on uncoated. When choosing a PMS color, be sure you're looking at a swatch printed on the kind of paper you'll be using for printing.

The procedure for indicating spot color on your mechanical is precisely the same as indicating a gray screen. Circle the colored area on your overlay and indicate the PMS color number you want. If you want a solid color text or tint block, write "100%" and the color name or number. You aren't limited to using solid colors, though — a colored ink can be screened to a percentage tint for different effects. In fact, using the same PMS-color ink in different percentage screens lets you pay for only one color ink but use several shades of that color in your design.

To indicate a screened color to the print shop, circle the area on the tracing paper overlay and write in the name or PMS number of the color you want and the percentage screen (in 10 percent increments). *Don't* print out the material you want reproduced in a tint using the tint screens provided by your page layout software. The type or shapes you want reproduced in tint should appear in solid black on your mechanical. The print shop will use that solid black shape to create the screened image.

Preseparating Colors

If you plan to use a substantial amount of spot color in your layout, consider printing a separate camera-ready page for each color you're using. In many page-layout programs you can indicate your color choice and have the program automatically print out separate pages. If yours doesn't, you can achieve the same effect by making an additional copy of the pages in question. Delete items until you have one page for each ink color.

Whichever technique you choose for preseparating colors, you will need registration marks on each camera-ready page to indicate precise alignment for the printer. Also remember to label each page with the color you want.

Also watch out for designs requiring pinpoint precision in registration. If two different colors touch, the commercial printer must position the printing plates with extraordinary care to avoid overlaps or unsightly gaps. Most commercial printers can handle this, but you may have to pay extra to achieve the required level of precision.

Check With Your Print Shop

What I've presented here are workable techniques for preparing mechanicals, handling illustrations, and indicating tint/color blocks, using basic desktop publishing software and an absolute minimum of manual dexterity. But these are not the only ways to get the job done.

Ask to see a mechanical prepared the way the print shop you're using likes to see them. There are dozens of idiosyncrasies in preparing mechanicals. The closer you conform to your printer's preferred system, the more likely it is that your job will be printed quickly and accurately.

CHAPTER 12

If I Knew Then...

When I was angry at myself for fouling something up as a kid, my parents' standard words of comfort were: "The important thing is to learn from your mistakes."

Now I give the same advice to my own kids. But I've also realized that there's something even better than learning from your mistakes — learning from *other people's* mistakes! After all, you still get the educational benefit, and you don't suffer the consequences of fouling up in the first place.

In that spirit, I've decided to end this book by describing some of the mistakes I've made in the process of learning desktop publishing, and point out ways you can do it smarter, easier, and less expensively than I did. Hey, what are friends for?

If I knew then what I know now, I would have...

...Reread My Software Manuals After a Few Months

When I start using a new desktop publishing program, I want to build a publication as soon as possible. That means absorbing just enough information from the manuals to accomplish the job at hand, and letting a lot of material just sort of wash over me in that initial flood of information.

The first things you lose in this initial quick reading of the manual, in my experience, are the shortcuts. It's easy to use a mouse and a pull-down menu. There may be keystroke combinations or software features that will get the job done faster, but they're harder to learn and remember than clicking on menu items, so you learn the mouse techniques first. And if you never go back to the manual, you'll probably never pick up those timesaving shortcuts.

...Purchased a Large-Screen Monitor Sooner

There's a danger in reviewing hardware for *Home Office Computing* magazine. Sometimes, when I'm done evaluating the equipment, it's painful having to send it back. The only alternative, though, is to dig deep and pay for the evaluation unit. That's what happened after writing a buyer's guide to large-screen portrait monitors — I bought the Princeton Publishing Labs MultiView unit I reviewed. And am I glad I did!

A portrait monitor displays a complete single page at virtually actual size. One advantage from a design perspective is the opportunity to see the entire page layout at once. After working with the monitor for a while, though, I realize the overwhelming benefit is the fact that I don't waste time scrolling around the page. If I need to make a change at the lower right corner of the page, I click the mouse there and start editing text or moving objects. If I then see a problem in the upper left, I click there and fix it. I didn't realize just how much time I was wasting scrolling the part of the page I needed onto the screen until I stopped having to do it.

Granted, we are talking about a significant investment here — in the $1,000 neighborhood including the monitor and the graphics card required to drive it. But I am not only doing a better job by working on full pages, I am saving time and eliminating tedium. According to my cost-benefit equation, that was money well spent.

...Chosen a Larger Hard Disk Right Away

Desktop publishing is a hard-disk-intensive undertaking. The page-layout programs themselves take up plenty of room. Downloadable fonts have a healthy appetite for hard disk space. And scanned images are absolute gluttons!

I started out with a 20-megabyte hard disk on my Macintosh and a 40-megabyte disk in my PC-compatible. Both were woefully inadequate. Now they have each been upgraded with 100-megabyte hard disks and, frankly, I could *still* use more room for my desktop publishing work and all the other tasks I undertake with my computer.

...Started Buying Software From Mail Order Suppliers Sooner

After buying all of my software from computer stores for several years, I finally decided to take a chance on mail order. After all, the advertised prices were a lot better than retail, and you couldn't beat the convenience. It was a good move on my part.

So far, my experience with mail order has been flawless. I haven't done an exhaustive study of the subject, but I can tell you that when I've ordered from MicroWarehouse (800-367-7080), PC Connection (800-243-8088) and MacConnection (800-334-4444) I've gotten prompt delivery of the latest version of the software, and paid substantially discounted prices.

...Avoided Buying Rarely Used Fonts

There are times when you need a particular typeface for a special purpose, and really don't expect to need it again before the return of Halley's Comet. Do you bite the bullet and buy the typeface package? I've done it in the past...but I've found a better way.

Actually, I have two better ways to recommend. The first is patronizing the Adobe forum on CompuServe (GO ADOBE to get there). In the Libraries section are screen fonts for the entire Adobe library in both PC-compatible and Macintosh formats, free for the downloading, along with instructions for installing them in your desktop publishing program.

What good are the screen fonts? You can't use them for printing final output (they don't provide adequate resolution). However, you can use them in your page-layout program for composing your publication (the spacing will be correct) and printing out proofs. Then, when it's time to produce final output for reproduction, find a computer-equipped quick-print shop (for laser-printer output) or a desktop publishing service bureau (for laser or imagesetter output) that has the font you've used installed on their system and bring them your disk.

Another option is to use the fonts provided with object-oriented drawing programs, and import the text you create as an illustration in your desktop publishing program. The champ in this category for my work has been *CorelDRAW*. It comes with a superb collection of typefaces, and will output to any device supported by Microsoft Windows, including HP LaserJet and PostScript formats. The program's typographic controls are extremely precise, and the results for headlines or the occasional block of body text are excellent. If you want to set a headline in Cooper Black, Friz Quadrata, Stencil, Tiffany, or some other typeface that isn't used often but is precisely right for special purposes, the *Corel* equivalents will serve you well.

...Kept Double or Triple Backup Copies of My Files

I wrote and desktop-published a 32-page booklet for an insurance company client. Delivered mechanicals. Got paid. Copied the files off my hard disk onto a floppy and stored it.

Six months later the phone rings. Insurance regulations have changed. They need minor revisions throughout the brochure. No problem. I quote them a low price, knowing there really isn't much work to be done. Take out the backup floppy. Insert in disk drive. Load publication. No dice. No way. Uh-uh. Perspire heavily. Try various disk-fixing utility programs. Forget it. For a perverse moment I thought I heard the disk drive laughing at me as the heads merrily skipped across the completely unreadable surface. I then sat down to re-create the entire booklet from scratch.

There's nothing special about my story, I suppose — everybody loses valuable files to magnetic gremlins. But it won't happen to me again. I now keep triple backups of important files.

Three copies? The impeccable logic behind this strategy came to me courtesy of *The Macintosh Bible* (published by Peachpit Press), a book of tips and techniques I heartily recommend. I quote: "Let's say you only have two copies of something and your disk drive screws up. You insert the first disk and see garbage on the screen. Naturally you assume there's something wrong with that disk, but you're not worried, because you have a second disk with the same document on it. So you insert the second disk and the drive zaps that too. At that point you realize the problem is with the drive, not the disk, but it's too late — unless you have a third copy."

...Typeset a Few Sample Pages First

For most of my work I use the laser printer for working proofs and send out for high-resolution Linotronic imagesetter output for mechanicals. However, there is plenty of room for error between laser-printer output and imagesetter results from the same file. This is especially true if you are working with a PC-compatible system and sending your files to a service bureau working with Macintosh equipment (which describes every service bureau I've encountered to date).

What kind of problems, you ask?

For instance, the thickness of the lines you use for boxes, intercolumn rules, and other design elements. The first time I encountered this problem I typeset an entire 24-page magazine, each page with fine hairline rules between the columns. Those rules looked just fine on the laser proofs, but nearly vanished in the imagesetter version. The reason — they were printing a single dot wide, and a single 300-dpi dot looks very different from a 1,270-dpi dot. The solution then was to manually paste laser-printed rules onto each page. The better answer was to adjust the program settings for 1,270-dpi resolution before printing to a file and sending the file to the service bureau. I could have learned the same lesson on a three-page sample run and saved myself gluey fingers and a missed deadline.

And remember that, even if nothing goes wrong at all, your imagesetter output will look different from the laser proof because the imagesetter type will be lighter and more detailed than the laser-printed version. Play it safe. Have some sample pages set.

...Started Using Disk Caching Sooner

Every time your desktop publishing software has to load information from your hard drive, it slows down the process of building pages. And it doesn't take many days watching that little red drive-activity light blinking at you to realize that desktop publishing is a hard-disk-intensive activity.

How do you cut down on the data-fetching crawl? Use disk-caching software. Unfortunately I spent two years watching that hard disk grind away before anyone explained disk caching to me.

A disk cache is an area of computer memory set aside to hold data you've already accessed. The next time you need the same data, the disk-caching software looks first in memory — if what you need is there, it loads from memory rather than loading from the hard drive. Loading from memory is much, much faster. And you'll find that your computer frequently *does* need to reread the same data over and over again.

A disk cache is different from a RAM disk. When you set up a RAM disk the computer treats a section of memory as if it were a real disk drive. It reads files from that area, but it also writes files to that area — and if you turn off the power before copying files in a RAM disk to a floppy or hard disk, those files are flushed down the electron stream. A disk cache, on the other hand, will read information from the cache but write changed files directly to the disk drive. Much safer.

My current choice for PC-compatible disk-caching software is *Super PC-Kwik* from Multisoft. It's fast, flexible, works well using its default settings, can be customized if you're into that, and has been entirely reliable. Microsoft Windows comes with its own caching program, but I'm happy with *PC-Kwik* performance for both my Windows and non-Windows programs.

Macintosh disk caching is a slightly different story. Caching capability is built into the system software — you turn it on or off and set the size using the Control Panel. But the Mac has the ability to make more memory available directly to the program, and that can improve software performance tremendously. I keep my Macintosh disk cache set at a modest size and let the programs have as much of the remaining RAM as they can use.

Enough of My Mistakes!

Now that I've shared a raft of information that I had to pick up bit by bit from diverse sources over time, and even opened my personal anxiety closet to reveal my mistakes in hopes you'll avoid them, all that's left is to wish you a profitable, enjoyable desktop publishing experience.

INDEX

COLOPHON

This book was designed and produced by the author, incorporating valuable suggestions from Kate Pferdner and Lydia Lewis at AMACOM.

Page layouts were created using *Personal Press* on a Macintosh IIsi computer. Working proofs were printed on an Apple LaserWriter IIf printer. Final camera-ready pages were output by APC Publishing Center in New York City on a Linotronic L300 image-setter at 1,270 dpi.

The body type, headings, and subheadings are set in Adobe Caslon in several weights and styles. Illustration captions are set in Adobe's Tekton Oblique and Tekton Regular typefaces.

Samples created using PC-compatible programs were output on a Hewlett-Packard LaserJet Series II printer equipped with the Adobe PostScript cartridge.

Illustrations incorporated in the book were taken from the libraries of the clip-art publishers featured in Chapter 6.

And incidentally, if you've been looking at the sample layouts and wondering what the heck "Lorem ipsum dolor sit amet" means, I assure you it is not the chant recited by the Druids before making a sacrifice to the Gods of Typography. "Lorem ipsum" etc. is a standard block of pseudo-Latin text used by designers to fill their sample layouts with type that looks real enough, but doesn't include actual words that might distract the viewer from concentrating on the design.